DO SPIES WIN OLYMPIC MEDALS?

SPORTS, GAMES AND GAMBLING

FASCINATING FACTS AND
EVERYDAY PHRASES EXPLAINED

Peter Ryding

PATHFINDER

Published by Pathfinder Partners Ltd.

ISBN 0-9551525-6-9
ISBN 978-0-9551525-6-6

Designed and illustrated by Oxford Designers & Illustrators

Cover design by Baseline Arts Ltd., Oxford

Printed and bound in Germany by GGP Media GmbH, Pößneck

For

Edward and Richard – the sportsmen!

Acknowledgements

I would like to take this opportunity to thank everyone who has so enthusiastically embraced and supported the WINKT project from its inception: the many dinner guests who have patiently listened, challenged and in some cases politely fallen asleep whilst I have shared my latest linguistic discoveries; Steve, the guy in the pub who challenged me to write the first book; Peter at ODI, who has been a stalwart supporter and always kept a sense of humour despite everything (and there have been lots of 'things'!); Nick, my artist; Gillian, who has challenged and checked and added her own ideas despite an apparently endless set of iterations.

Of the many others, who are too many to fit on one page but who have encouraged me throughout, I would like to thank Crisspy the Duck and his friends, Simon, Neil, Spence, Tim (Nadia), Sam (Jo), Hutch, Gordon, Alexander The Great and Henry V, all of whom have played their roles, plus the designer of the keel of the boat, without whom we would all have drowned.

Also thanks to the many members of WINKT the club who continue to write in with both intriguing questions and fascinating discoveries.

Thanks to every one of you.

Contents

Preface

Imagine you are a foreigner who has just learnt the basics of the English language. You proudly walk into a room of native English speakers and listen to their conversation.

'Was it a cock-up you ask? I should bally say so! But it's a good job he had an extra string to his bow because they had him running from pillar to post in that job. His boss's ideas were so off the wall that it wound him up something proper. No wonder he's legged it!'

You may well think you had been on the wrong course!

But it's not just the phrases we use that make English tough to learn and a joy to use. Our language has absorbed more subtleties and richness from other nations than any other. Indeed, English is by far the most widely used official language in the world. We also have the largest vocabulary in the world, at over 250,000 words in the *Oxford English Dictionary*. Having said that, we each tend to pick from our own favourite 2–3,000 most of the time, rarely stepping outside our comfort zone. To put this into context, Shakespeare used over 21,000 words and a top scrabble player will know over 80,000 words!

So, with all this richness and precision at our fingertips, such that we can intuitively distinguish between a simple 'room' and a grander 'chamber' (in a way that many languages cannot), what do we do? We dredge up obscure phrases that often arose for reasons that are no longer relevant and that people don't really understand anyway. Or, even worse, ones that they misunderstand. For example, imagine the foreigner who overhears that something is 'cheap at half the price'. What does that mean? Is it saying that it would be cheap if it was half the current price? In other words, that it is expensive? Or is it saying that it is cheap because it is half the price you were expecting to pay? If *we* are not sure – what chance do foreigners have?

In many cases phrases have simply gone wrong over the ages. For example, take 'the exception that proves the rule'. Pardon? Are we saying that finding an exception to a rule somehow proves that the rule is correct? Surely that has to be utter tosh!

It is only through patient research and an understanding of our heritage that we can make sense of such expressions. In this case the explanation goes back to the Normans' invasion of England in 1066 and their desire to have a clear set of rules with which they could govern the country. The trouble was that the barely literate Anglo-Saxons had few written laws. Most were simply 'known' to those who dispensed justice. However, the Normans passed a law that said that if someone could prove beyond doubt that there was an exception to a law, then by implication that would prove, in another case, that the law did exist. For example, a trader who had a pass allowing him to travel at night after the curfew hour – literally, the hour at which the fire (*feu*) had to be covered (*couvert*) – would prove that the law of curfew did exist. This in turn would enable the

prosecution of someone who broke the curfew. Hence, an exception to a rule does not in fact prove that the rule is correct. However, it does prove that the rule exists!

Yet another example of things going wrong is the phrase 'Don't spoil the ship for a hap'orth of tar!' Now, tar may be cheap, but a hap'orth (that's half a penny's worth for those born after 1980) of it does not go far when you are trying to waterproof an entire ship! In fact, by digging into the past we discover that the saying originally referred not to a ship at all but rather to a humble *sheep*! The reason is that just about the only help you could give a sheep with an open sore or wound was to slap on a dollop of tar. This would at

least close the wound and was of course worth doing – especially given the financial value of sheep in medieval days, when they produced the vast majority of England's income. After all, without them we could not have afforded to fight the French through the Hundred Years War! And let's face it, you don't often get the chance to humiliate the entire French nation like we did at the battles of Crécy, Poitiers and Agincourt! Well worth a hap'orth of tar so that we don't spoil the *sheep*!

However, the story is not all mistakes and misunderstandings. Some derivations are a sheer joy to discover. Like the Greek god who used to jump out on humans and scare them away

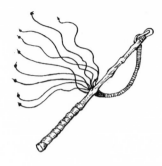

from his personal harem of nymphs and dryads. His name was Pan, from which we get the word PANIC! Or the need for sailors to be flogged up on the main deck because down below in the cramped conditions there was NOT ENOUGH ROOM TO SWING A CAT – o' nine tails! Why nine tails? Because the Royal Navy decided that the normal three-headed scourge representing the Father, the Son and the Holy Ghost was not 'holy enough' for wicked sailors and so created a 'trinity of holy trinities'. Hence nine tails that left deep scratches on the skin just like the claws of a CAT. And of course the scars would then stay with the troublemaker for the rest of his life, making him a MARKED MAN!

There is also the wonderful realization that so often when different words sound similar they are in fact the same word,

or at least come from the same original source. For example, cheque books, checkmate in chess, checklists, rain checks, the checks (bills) you get in American restaurants, the game of chequers, checkered patterns, the Chancellor of the Exchequer, Chequers pub signs, the prime minister's country house Chequers and simply 'checking something out', all derive from medieval military coups in Persia! Wonderful!

Having studied our language hand in hand with our history for over two decades, I am still surprised, amazed and delighted at what treasures I uncover on a regular basis. Creating this series of books has been a massive and painstaking undertaking, bringing a lot of pleasure and at times a lot of frustration. I just hope that you have fun with the books and that you will find something fascinating, insightful and intriguing within each book that makes you say 'Well, I Never Knew That!' And of course, when you do, please tell your friends and join WINKT the club at www.winkt.com – and vote for WINKT to become a new word in the English language! Thank you for doing so.

Don't just enjoy the English language – CREATE IT!

How to use this book

This book has been written in a unique format so that you can enjoy it in several different ways:

1. You can **read it cover to cover** as an adventure into the rich stories and interconnectedness behind our language.

2. You can **flick to a page** and discover fascinating facts bit by bit.

3. You can **study the pictures** at the start of each chapter and try to work out the sayings that await you inside.

4. You can **seek out specific words** and sayings via the index.

5. You can **use it as a quiz book** on your own or spoken out loud with friends, by reading each paragraph and then stopping just before the CAPITALS reveal the answers.

6. You can just leave it in the loo for everyone to enjoy. But beware – your guests may not come out for some time! And, of course, when they do they are bound to say – **'Well, I Never Knew That!'**

1

Ancient Greece and the Olympics

The gods were part of every aspect of life in ancient Greece and so perhaps it is not surprising that we owe many of our everyday phrases and the world's most international sporting event to the Greek gods and the mortals with whom they played.

Well, I never knew that . . .
. . . a female athlete created the Olympic Games, yet women
were not allowed to compete!

In Greek mythology Atlanta was a beautiful and athletic maiden who had been raised in the wild by a bear. She worshipped the moon and could run faster than any mortal being. Her beauty attracted many suitors but she rejected them all. Eventually, in an attempt to discourage them, she offered to marry any man who could outrun her. The only condition was that anyone who failed would be put to death. The goddess Aphrodite, lover of the sun god Apollo, gave one of his followers, Hippomenes, three golden apples. Hippomenes then challenged Atlanta to a race. As he ran he dropped the apples and Atlanta stopped to pick them up. Consequently he won the race and married her. In celebration, and to give thanks to the gods, they established a festival of running races at the base of the mountain upon which the gods lived – Mount Olympus. This event became known as the OLYMPIC GAMES. Over time other sports were incorporated and other locations started their own versions of

the games. Ironically, given how the Olympics came about, women were not allowed to compete in the ancient Olympic Games, partially because all competitors were naked! Although perhaps the men were really afraid of losing to Atlanta's descendants!

Now, the Greeks used an eight-year calendar based upon the fact that every eight years the moon and the sun, and for that matter the planet Venus, came almost exactly into phase with each other. Four of the sporting festivals established themselves as the premier events and they each took turns in attracting competitors from across Greece. To fit in with the calendar each festival took place twice every eight years. This is why the Olympic Games are still held only ONCE EVERY FOUR YEARS. In fact, reflecting the significance of these sporting festivals, the Greeks then switched from their eight-year calendar to one of four years and called it the Olympiad calendar.

Well, I never knew that . . .
. . . you can't rest on your laurels if you start from scratch

One of the other three sporting celebrations was held in honour of the god Apollo at Pythia. As the bay tree, a member of the laurel family, was closely associated with Apollo, the winners would be awarded crowns made from the ends of the branches, literally 'WINNING THE LAURELS'. Related expressions refer to the need to strive for further success even after having been successful – 'DON'T REST ON YOUR LAURELS' – and to focus upon the prize as a form of motivation: 'LOOK TO YOUR LAURELS'.

In ancient Greece, *stade* was the word for a pace. Races were named using the number of paces involved (100 stade, 500 stade, etc.). Eventually the word became strongly associated with the 200-stade race (around 190 metres). As many sports-related amphitheatres had such a race track designed into them, they became known as *stadions,* a word that we use in its Latinized version: STADIUM.

A mark scratched in the ground was often used as the starting point of a running race. In handicap races some people would start ahead of this line. Others would START FROM SCRATCH.

Well, I never knew that . . .
. . . spying is actually an Olympic sport

Towards the end of the 4th century AD Rome was under constant attack from barbarians. The Empire adopted Christianity as its official religion in an attempt to galvanize the population against the pagan attacks. In fact in AD 394 the Emperor called Theodosius (literally meaning 'Friend of

God') banned all non-Christian festivals. This included sporting celebrations based around the ancient Greek gods, and so all the religious sporting events, such as the Olympics, ceased.

Then, in 1896, after a gap of over 1,500 years, the Frenchman Pierre de Coubertin, a sportsman and physical fitness fanatic, reintroduced the major international sporting festival from ancient Greece into the modern sporting calendar. He called it THE MODERN OLYMPIC GAMES. These new games were designed to encourage involvement from all countries across all five continents linked together in harmony. To represent this ideal, and to ensure that every country felt involved, the

symbol became FIVE INTERLOCKING RINGS with colours that (at the time) included at least one colour of every national flag sending a competitor – RED, GREEN, BLUE, YELLOW, BLACK AND THE WHITE BACKGROUND. Refreshingly for a Frenchman, he also fought for the RIGHT OF WOMEN TO COMPETE.

The Greeks considered fire to be mystical and very holy. According to legend it had been stolen from Zeus and given to humankind by Prometheus. Consequently, throughout the ancient Olympic Games a fire was kept burning at the temple of Zeus. Incidentally, this was the location of a massive ivory and gold statue that was one of the Seven Wonders of the World – THE STATUE OF ZEUS AT OLYMPIA. In the 1928 Olympics this tradition of a flame was reintroduced and then in 1936 the Germans introduced the idea of a flaming torch taking the flame from Mount Olympus to the Olympic stadium in Berlin. Ever since, all Olympic Games have included both the OLYMPIC TORCH RELAY from Olympus and the OLYMPIC FIRE burning throughout the games. Ironically, the first torches used for this purpose were supplied by Krupp, a German arms manufacturer that made guns and ammunition for the German army in both world wars and so indirectly led to the cancelling of the Olympics in 1916, 1940 and 1944, when it was not practical to hold them because of the disruptions caused by the conflicts. Interestingly, though, in ancient Greece all wars stopped for the Olympic Games and competitors were given safe passage even through enemy territories. Who says we are becoming more civilized?

Now, because the Olympics were cancelled in 1916, 1940 and 1944, only 25 modern Olympic Games have been held. However, in true ancient *Olympiad calendar* style the modern Olympics are numbered by how many sets of four years have elapsed from the first modern Olympic Games in 1896. Hence, even though it was actually the 25th modern event that actually took place, the 2004 Olympic Games in Athens was called the 28TH MODERN OLYMPIAD.

In 1912 Baron de Coubertin created a new Olympic sport based upon a romantic 19th-century concept. The idea was that a spy is riding through enemy territory when his horse is shot and he has to defend himself with sword and gun. He then escapes by swimming over a river and runs back to his camp. The sport includes horse-riding, fencing, shooting, swimming and running, and is called THE MODERN PENTATHLON. The ancient Olympics also had a pentathlon that was based upon sports that are all still in the competition

individually: throwing the javelin, throwing the discus, running (although then it was in full armour!), jumping and wrestling (then it was naked).

Well, I never knew that . . .
. . . a no holds barred fight could put you in agony

Agon was an old Greek word for an assembly of people. This was applied to the ancient Olympic Games and other

11

sporting gatherings where large numbers of people would assemble to watch competitors exert themselves to their limits, and in some cases try to force submissions, as for example in wrestling. From this we get the word AGONY. The winning competitors were called *agonistes*. When two fought, the prefix *anti* (meaning against) would be used to describe the challenger – from which we get our word ANTAGONIST.

Over time, various regulations were introduced into wrestling to reduce severe or permanent injuries to contestants by banning, for example, eye-gouging or holds that could break an arm. These eventually became highly formalized into strict codes of rules. However, many spectators preferred to see more vicious fights and would pay extra to see illegal matches in which there were no constraints on what the wrestlers could do. These fights were described as NO HOLDS BARRED.

Well, I never knew that . . .
. . . Pheidippides should have got a trophy for
running 140 miles!

In 490 BC an Athenian messenger named Pheidippides (sometimes written as Philippides) ran the 140 miles from Athens to Sparta in just 48 hours, to seek the Spartans' help against an invading Persian army. Unfortunately the Spartans were in the middle of a very important religious festival and they refused to march until the forthcoming full moon. Pheidippides ran back with the message. With a Persian fleet approaching the city of Athens the massively outnumbered Athenian army marched over 20 miles to the Persian camp on the nearby plain of Marathon and bravely charged the entire Persian army. To everyone's surprise the Athenians defeated them!

Meanwhile the Persian fleet was moving to attack Athens itself and the Athenian civilians were preparing to abandon the city and flee to the north. It was vital that they were told of their army's victory before they let the Persians in, and so a messenger (some say it was Pheidippides again) was sent to Athens to announce the victory in order to ensure that the population did not lose hope and surrender the city. He ran the whole distance from the battlefield to Athens, which has since been measured as 24.85 miles, without stopping. According to legend, upon arrival he had the strength for just one word, 'Niki!', meaning 'Victory!' (hence also the sporting brand name – NIKE), and then, sadly, he died as a result of his exertions.

From this heroic feat we get the modern-day race that was initially exactly 24.85 miles long. However, in the London

Olympics of 1908 the Queen wished the race to start from Windsor Castle and finish at the Olympic stadium in the area of London known as White City. This was over a mile further than the accepted distance of 24.85 miles. No sooner had the new distance been agreed than the Queen asked that the race finish right in front of her in the royal box in the stadium. This brought the whole distance to 26 miles and 385 yards. Ever since, this has become the internationally approved official distance of the MARATHON RACE. In fact, for many years after this there was an ironic tradition of shouting 'God bless the Queen!' at the 24-mile marker. From the incredible exertions needed to complete such a race we also get the phrase for any long and very testing challenge – A MARATHON. **WINKT!**

2

Gladiators and Other Roman Sports

The Romans worked and fought hard, but they played even harder! In fact our modern sportsmen, fans and hooligans are nothing compared to those of the Roman chariot races and the gladiatorial arena.

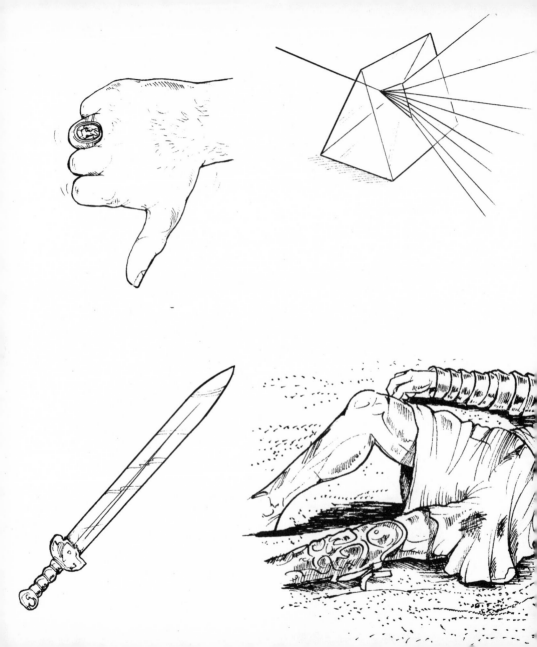

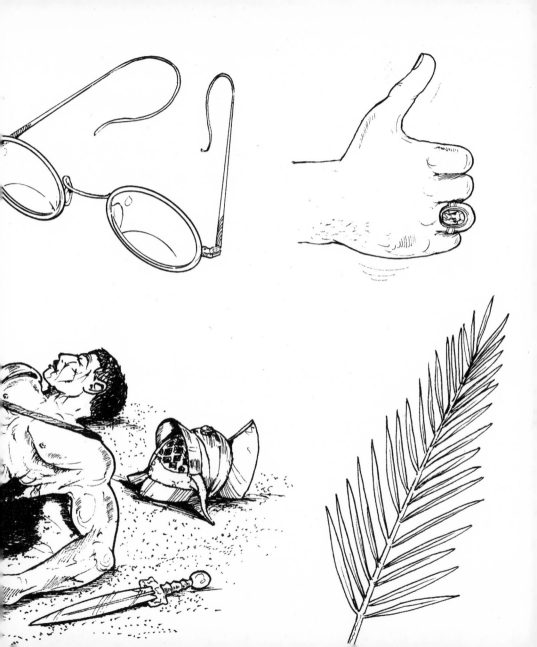

Well, I never knew that . . .

. . . some Roman ladies gave gladiators the thumbs up

R oman generals armed their soldiers with the famous short stabbing sword – the gladius. They did this to stop them taking wild swings and instead make them operate as a team, stabbing out from behind a wall of shields into the exposed armpits of their enemies who were taking big swings. There is even conjecture that some generals did not allow their soldiers to sharpen the sides of their blades, further discouraging any cutting swings. This was also the sword often used in arenas when slaves fought each other to the death. These competitors were named after the sword: GLADIATORS.

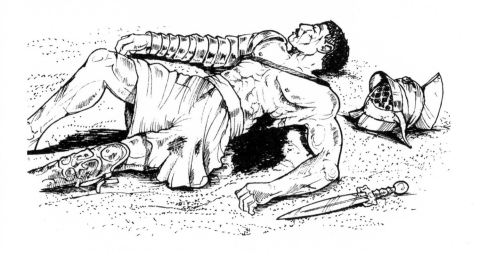

Many of these gladiators were criminals, prisoners of war or simply people who had fallen out with the emperor. They would be shoved into the arena and have to fight for their lives in a bizarre range of contests. Christians were often pitted against wild animals such as lions or even maddened elephants from North Africa. Incidentally, the Romans called black panthers 'pards'. They also assumed that the animals that resembled yellow lions but had black spots on them were in fact a cross between lions and panthers. Hence the name that we still use: LEOPARDS.

Sometimes one man would be made to wear a helmet with no eye-holes so that he could not see his opponent. Sometimes women would be set against dwarves. One emperor even personally fought against opponents who were weakened through drugs and lack of food and had to use weapons made of lead so that they could hardly be picked up! He is recorded has having had over 200 successful fights!

There were also professional gladiators trained to use specific sets of weapons, who would rarely be killed simply because they cost so much to train and look after. A few of these would become celebrities, like modern-day football stars, and occasionally would earn their freedom by being so popular that they were liberated by the Emperor. These gladiators were fine physical specimens and would often attract rich female admirers who would visit the gladiatorial barracks for a 'bit of rough' and pay for the privilege.

If two professional gladiators gave a good display of skilled and exciting fighting, the crowd would give a symbol that the loser should be spared. The ultimate decision was made by the Emperor, who would often assess the mood of the audience and then usually follow their lead. To save someone he would make a fist with his right hand held sideways and then extend his thumb, which then became representative of the victorious gladiator's sword. He would then twist his wrist to make his thumb point either upwards, meaning he would live, or downwards, meaning the sword should be thrust into the losing gladiator's heart. Hence we get the gesture and verbal expression THUMBS UP – and, of course, THUMBS DOWN!

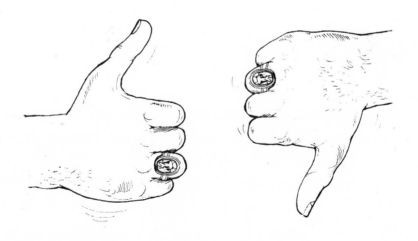

Well, I never knew that . . .
. . . the Romans gave us Oxford Circus!

Ruling the Roman Empire was obviously a very difficult business, and the emperors consistently feared uprisings and coups that would oust them, almost certainly with calamitous results for both them and their families. The commentator Juvenal said in the 2nd century that there are primarily two things an emperor has to give the population to keep it happy: food, and thrilling entertainment such as chariot races and gladiator games, which would take place in round amphitheatres called *circuses*. Hence the phrase meaning giving people basic food and entertainment to keep them from thinking about other more important things: BREAD AND CIRCUSES. This is where we get the term for a show involving horses and other acts going around and around an arena to entertain the audience: CIRCUS. It is also why many junctions in central London, where at some time in the past there has been some form of roundabout, are also called circuses. Examples include Oxford Circus, where Oxford Street intersects with Regent Street, and Cambridge Circus, where

Shaftesbury Avenue and other roads intersect. The Latin word for 'sand' has given us an alternative name for a sports stadium. Originally, however, it was applied only to those amphitheatres where gladiators or Christians would be killed in large numbers, and where in fact the sand was needed to soak up the blood: ARENA (Latin for 'sand').

In ancient Rome, palm leaves were a sign of deep respect and admiration. This is why Jesus' path into Jerusalem was paved with palm leaves, giving the Christian celebration of

Palm Sunday. Equally, a victorious gladiator would be given a palm leaf in recognition of his achievement: hence the expression TO BEAR A PALM. Notable gladiators could eventually win their freedom, and this would be signified by the award of a *rudis*, a wooden sword. But many of these gladiators still went on taking part in the contests, not wanting to give up the fame, the lifestyle and the buzz of the adrenalin rush.

Well, I never knew that . . .
. . . the Romans gave us spectacles!

Towards the end of the Roman Empire the sport of charioteering became an obsession with many people. In fact the Circus Maximus was a specially built racing circuit designed to accommodate over 200,000 people – around 15 per cent of the entire population of Rome. Initially there were two teams: *russata* (red) and *albata* (white). When the contests were expanded to include two more chariots per race, the *passina* (green) and *veneta* (blue) teams emerged. This sport became far more important than football or Formula One in contemporary British society and led to political affiliations and vicious riots. The word used to describe these various teams has come to be used in political and other arenas in the modern world: FACTIONS. In fact, the rioting and disquiet caused by these warring factions was a contributor to the overall decline and fall of the Roman Empire. Now there's a warning for football fans!

The arenas that were specially built for these races, in which the chariots were drawn by horses, were often named after the Greek word for horse, *hippos*, and *dromos*, meaning 'course': HIPPODROME. The association with large crowds, excitement and big venues has led to old-style music halls, theatres and night clubs adopting this name. Many of them in fact took the name of the world's largest ever 'colossal' arena for gladiatorial combat: THE COLOSSEUM, often spelt COLISEUM.

 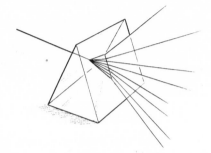

Spectare, meaning to watch, has given us our words for people who watch, SPECTATORS, and for devices to help us watch, SPECTACLES; also for the splitting of light into its full range of colours, SPECTRUM, and hence for a full set of variations of anything: FULL SPECTRUM. Then again, there is our word for a 'must-see event', a SPECTACLE, which will inevitably prove to be SPECTACULAR. The viewing of something from a particular angle gives us the word ASPECT. Combining *spectare* with the prefix *sub-* meaning 'under', we get the word meaning someone who appears to be taking a sneaky look at something: SUSPECT (subspect); and anyone who suspects someone else is SUSPICIOUS. **WINKT!**

3

Football – Rugby, Soccer and NFL

Football today is big business, with
club, national and international
teams, heroes and celebrities. But
this was not always the case . . .
in fact, it used to be illegal!

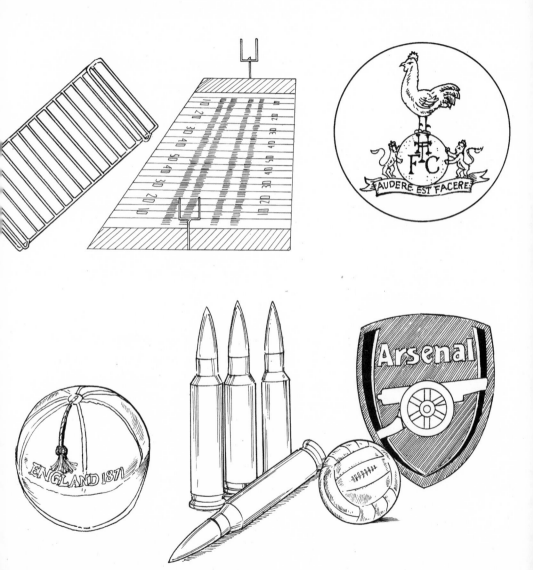

Well, I never knew that . . .
. . . medieval footballers were keener on fighting
each other than the enemy

Early football games consisted of boys and men from each of two neighbouring villages trying to kick or carry an inflated pig's bladder into the centre of the other village. Hence the game would be played over miles of ditches, hedges and woods. There were no rules, so fighting and injury were commonplace. It became so popular that during the Hundred Years War against France, football was

banned to ensure that young men practised with the new 'knight-beating' longbow. However, the law was often ignored and football never died out completely. By the 18th century it was very popular again and played on small fields with no handling of the ball allowed.

Then in 1823 a boy called William Webb-Ellis at a Midlands public school supposedly picked up the football and ran with it. This move was then incorporated into a local version of the game that became very popular and was named after the school: RUGBY. In fact, the Rugby World Cup trophy is named after this boy: the WEBB-ELLIS CUP.

In 1845 a group of ex-Rugby schoolboys who were practising medicine in London formed the first official football club and named it after the institution where they were working: Guy's Hospital Football Club. The Blackheath Rugby Club was founded 13 years later, and this remains the oldest continuously playing club in England. At this stage each club used its own version of the rules and arguments were common. So Blackheath helped form a new coordinating body for the sport which was called the FOOTBALL ASSOCIATION. However, many clubs did not want to allow handling of the ball or various 'hacking' moves, and so Blackheath and several other clubs that did want to play by these rules left the FA. In 1871 these breakaway clubs formed a new body to standardize the 'rugby' rules. This was called the RUGBY FOOTBALL UNION.

Well, I never knew that . . .

. . . in some games, just trying to score can win you points

But more disputes quickly arose in the new RFU. By 1895 acrimonious arguments had broken out between the northern working-class rugby clubs and the mainly middle- and upper-class southern rugby clubs. The working-class clubs formed a league in which players were paid and called themselves the Northern Rugby Football Union – renamed in 1922 the more familiar RUGBY LEAGUE. The other clubs retained the name Rugby Union and up until 1995 were technically not permitted to be paid as professionals. In reality ways were found around this rule: a compromise the press referred to as 'shamateurism'. The feelings stirred up by the split were so strong that anyone who switched from Union to League was automatically banned from ever playing Union again!

While the Rugby League rules have changed relatively little, Rugby Union rules have continued to evolve, introducing various elements that do not form part of Rugby League. In fact, the rules of Rugby League encourage getting the ball and running straight at the opposing players. This demands enormous strength, endurance and courage, and requires different team members to take their turns. This gives us a phrase reflecting this approach, meaning that everyone must play their role: 'PICK UP THE BALL AND RUN WITH IT!'

In the early days of rugby the only way to score points was by kicking the ball between the goalposts. However, if one team carried the ball over the opponents' back line, they were allowed to place the ball in front of the goal and *try* to score without any opponents getting in the way. Hence this was called a TRY. Subsequently it was decided that simply winning a try should score points. As these points could then be *converted* to a higher score if the team went on to score the goal as well, the goal became known as a CONVERSION. Incidentally, when a penalty is awarded the kicker must drop the ball onto the ground before kicking it; hence this is called a DROP KICK and, if the player scores, the goal is called a DROP GOAL.

In 1871 the English and Scottish national rugby teams held the first ever international match at Edinburgh. It was seen as a real *test* of the two proud nations and each put forward its very best team. Ever since then, recurring 'grudge' matches between the top sides have been referred to as TESTS or TEST MATCHES – a phrase subsequently adopted by other sports. After the match the players were given cloth caps as mementoes of the match – hence the phrase for playing in the national teams: being CAPPED.

In 1876 the colonial football club in Calcutta, India, was closed down and all the proceeds (silver rupees) were melted down and formed into a cup as a memento of the colonial game. This was then sent back to the Rugby Football Union in England. It was decided that this would be a fitting trophy for the new England–Scotland test match, and ever since this contest has been called the CALCUTTA CUP.

In the 1880s Wales and Ireland (which at the time was wholly within the United Kingdom) joined England and Scotland in what was called the Home International Championship.

Technically Wales is a principality and not a kingdom, while the other three are (or used to be) kingdoms in their own right, and so, to this day, if one such team beats all the other three it is said to have won the 'TRIPLE CROWN'. With the increasing militarization of Germany at the start of the 20th century France was invited to join this competition, and from 1910 it was renamed the FIVE NATIONS. In 2000 Italy joined as well, creating the current SIX NATIONS. When a team beats all five other teams in this competition, the achievement is referred to using an old bridge term that means to win all 13 tricks: a GRAND SLAM. The team that comes last in this competition gets an award derived from an old Cambridge University custom, originally given for the worst maths score each year – the WOODEN SPOON. In 2005, Wales beat all five other teams and so won the Grand Slam and the Triple Crown. Italy received the wooden spoon.

Rugby Union is now played in over a hundred countries worldwide, with Australia, New Zealand and South Africa competing in the TRI-NATIONS and then every four years a global competition being held for the RUGBY WORLD CUP.

In 1866 the Hampstead Football Club was formed but 14 years later there were serious internal disputes and the club split in two – neither being able to use the old name. However, one group decided to adopt a name that would enable it to keep using the old HFC monogram on its kit, stationery, etc. They opened the dictionary at the letter 'H' and almost immediately found a word that conveyed lightness afoot. They immediately change their name to the HARLEQUINS and soon after adopted the now famous Harlequin colours. In January 2006 Harlequins Rugby Union Football Club made history by agreeing to share its grounds with a Rugby League club that adopted the same name – Harlequins Rugby League – and the same distinctive colours!

Well, I never knew that . . .
. . . a tighthead prop might find himself in a grand slam
of heads

Because rugby initially allowed tripping and many other aggressive physical moves it was likened to the old inter-

village football *skirmishes,* and the formal face-offs became known by a word still used in the American form of rugby, American football: the SCRIMMAGE LINE. In British rugby the term became SCRUMMAGE, often shortened to SCRUM.

American football has evolved into a game in which, ironically, the ball very rarely comes into contact with a player's foot! In fact, scoring a 'goal' by kicking scores only one point, whereas achieving a 'touchdown' scores six points.

By comparison, in Rugby League, a try scores four points and a conversion two points.

Another indication of the common roots of rugby and American football is that in Rugby League the ball is handed over to the opposition after six attacking plays. In American football this happens after four attacking plays – unless the team has advanced 10 yards or more, in which case they start a new set of four plays. Interestingly, in Rugby Union, and of course soccer, no such rule exists.

There are other links between American football and the British game. Up to the Second World War in Canada their game was still referred to as RUGBY. Also, in American football and Rugby Union the players who are behind the scrum and scrimmage lines are call BACKS. The positions quarter back, half back and full back indicate how far towards the very back they play. In fact, while rugby position names seem impenetrable to the uninitiated they actually help explain the game.

The scrum is built around the player whose job it is to grapple with his opposite number and try to *hook* the ball out with his heel. He is called the HOOKER. He is supported and *propped* up by a player on each side, who are called the PROPS. These three form the front line of the scrum. When they engage with the opponents, their heads go between their opponents' heads, so that one prop has his head wedged between the heads of two opponents – he is called the TIGHTHEAD PROP. The other has his head touching one opponent's head and is loose on the other side. Hence he is called the LOOSEHEAD PROP.

The next row of the scrum is there to *lock* the first row firmly in position, so the two players here are both called LOCKS. Each side or *flank* of the scrum is covered by another player, both called FLANKERS. At the very back of the scrum, providing more 'oomph' and also trying to back-heel the ball out of the scrum, is the eighth man, called NUMBER EIGHT – and indeed he always wears number eight on his shirt. These men are collectively called forwards, and need to be big, tough and strong men, as opposed to the players behind, who are called backs and whose job it is to run very fast and nimbly, to duck and dive and to kick the ball forward. This is different from many sports (such as soccer), where the 'backs' tend to be the bigger, less nimble players. The two backs immediately behind the scrum are only halfway to the back of the team and so are called HALF BACKS. The one who takes the ball from the scrum is called the SCRUM HALF, and the one whose job it is to get the ball *flying* on to the rest of the team is called the FLY HALF. You then have two CENTRE BACKS; one out on each *wing*, the WINGERS; and one player who is right at the back of the team, called the FULL BACK.

American football has always been a game of strategy and tactics, with considerable planning put into preparation for each game and for every 'play' within each game. From this we get two phrases now used more widely, especially in business: MAKE A PLAY and GAME PLAN.

The markings on an American football pitch have been likened to the metal grids used for cooking food, and so it is often referred to as the GRIDIRON.

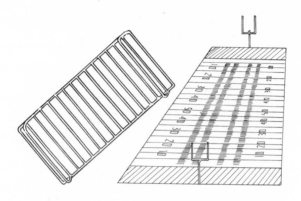

Incidentally, in the early days of motor racing metal gridirons would sometimes be placed in the ground where the cars started to give a better grip in muddy conditions. From this we get the term STARTING GRID.

In 1907 William Williams, a keen supporter of the game of rugby, bought a large old market garden in Twickenham, south London, to build a rugby ground. The ground is affectionately known as TWICKERS – and also sometimes as BILLY WILLIAMS' CABBAGE PATCH. In fact the nearest pub is still called THE CABBAGE PATCH. Rugby is a muddy game, and if a player is not playing well or is injured and is replaced during the match he can go off and clean up. This gives us a phrase meaning having not done well: TAKING AN EARLY BATH!

Well, I never knew that . . .
. . . Shakespeare would have been a Spurs fan

Shortly after Blackheath had led the Rugby rules football clubs out of the Football Association in the late 19th century, some university teams trendily abbreviated the word 'association' to 'socca', a name which was then taken up by other clubs, giving us our term SOCCER.

One of the first football clubs in the world was formed in 1865 in a northern pub called the Clinton Arms. The team was already playing a type of hockey but decided to switch to football and called themselves Forest Football Club. We now know them as NOTTINGHAM FOREST FOOTBALL CLUB.

Twenty years later a couple of ex-Forest players, including the goalie, were working in the royal ammunition factory in Woolwich and set up a new team, which they named after one of their workshops, 'Dial Square'. But they had no money, so they asked their old club for help. This arrived in the form of spare red football shirts and a ball. They have worn red ever since. Soon afterwards the club was renamed Woolwich Arsenal FC. When the chairman moved them to a better catchment area in north London (against protests from the existing north London club Tottenham Hotspur) in 1913 they dropped the Woolwich and became ARSENAL Football Club. The new ground was, of course, HIGHBURY.

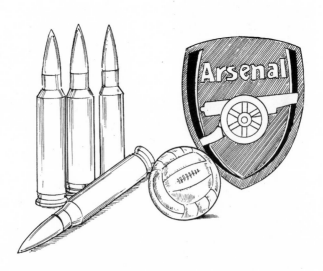

In 1882 a group of old boys from a north London grammar school added football to their existing cricket club's repertoire for the winter season. The part of London that they played in was named after an old Saxon chief called Totta, who had ruled the area before the Norman invasion of 1066. Subsequently the land had come under the control of the Percy family, one of the most powerful noble families in England. In the early 15th century one of the young Percys, Harry, was famous for always spurring his horse into the midst of battles. He was chosen to train the then Prince Henry (later to be King Henry V, the victor at Agincourt) in the art of combat and warfare. Ironically he then turned rebel and tried, unsuccessfully, to overthrow the royal family. He appears as a character in Shakespeare's *Henry IV*, nicknamed to reflect his bravery and headstrong nature: HARRY HOTSPUR. The Percys retained ownership of the land in north London for centuries, and eventually this connection was added to the name of the football club, which we know as TOTTENHAM HOTSPUR, called by its fans simply SPURS. 'Ham', incidentally, is an old English word for a home, group of houses or farm, so Totten-ham is literally the home or farm of Totta. The two

lions on the coat of arms of the club come directly from the coat of arms of the Percy family. The motto also reflects the character of Harry Hotspur: *Audere est facere,* meaning 'to dare is to do'. The famous cockerel symbol reflects the many cockpits that were located in London when cockfighting was one of the most popular sports in England, the link being that these fighting birds not only symbolized the fighting spirit but were armed with metal spikes on the back of their legs which were also called SPURS.

In 1878 the dining-room committee of the carriage and wagon works of the Lancashire and Yorkshire Railway Company formed a sports club that they called Newton

Heath Lancashire & Yorkshire Railway Cricket and Football Club. Twenty-four years later it went bankrupt. A new club was formed and named after the city in which it was based: MANCHESTER UNITED.

In 1892 Everton football club fell out with the landlord of its ground and ended up leaving, moving to a new ground at Goodison Park. The landlord was left with no income and so he formed a new club; he tried to reclaim the name Everton for it, but failed. Instead he named the club after the city: LIVERPOOL FC. The ground, of course, was ANFIELD.

'Cob' was an old English word for a lump. Hence the breed of swan with a black lump on its beak is the COB SWAN, and a head of maize with a lump at the centre is CORN ON THE COB. We also have a hemispherical loaf – a COB LOAF – a 'lumpy' hazelnut – COB NUT – and lumpy stones in the ground – COBBLESTONES. The old name for a spider, which has a large lump of a body, was also COB, from which we get COBWEB. The word 'cob' then developed to a slightly different spelling meaning a 'lump' of soil or a small hill. It is often heard at football pitches to describe the raised areas or gradients for fans that are now often converted into stands and historically called THE COP. Perhaps the most famous was at Liverpool, where it was spelt in the Dutch fashion: THE KOP. This is because it was named after a hill in South Africa where many Liverpudlians died in a battle.

In 1905 Fulham FC turned down the chance to rent a nearby sports ground. The owner of the ground was then approached by Great Western Railways, who wanted to develop the land. Fortunately he turned the offer down, and the ground was adopted by a new club. While the ground was technically in the borough of Hammersmith and Fulham, the team named themselves after another nearby London borough – CHELSEA. The ground is named after the nearby bridge over the river Stam – STAMFORD BRIDGE.

Football cup finals used to be held at a large south London sports ground. This caused some difficulties for the company that owned the ground when it wanted to create its own club, as other clubs claimed it was unfair. However, in 1905 it succeeded and used the cup final ground as its own until the First World War. Its name was Crystal Palace.

In the 1986 soccer World Cup in Mexico the spectators of several games amused themselves before matches by standing up and down in a way that created a ripple effect around the stadium. This had been seen five years before at a baseball match in America, but this was the first time that the rest of the world had seen it on TV. It became known after the location of the championship as THE MEXICAN WAVE. Incidentally, tests have shown that it needs about 15 people to stand up together to start a wave, and such waves typically travel at around 25 mph.

An invention to aid fair play was first seen on a football pitch in 1937. Its critical dimension is 10 yards, measured from the penalty spot. It is the 'D' or 'ARC' drawn at a 10-yard radius from the penalty spot on the outside of the goal area to keep opponents away from the penalty taker.

In Melbourne, Australia, an army barracks was situated very close to a football pitch and the colourful, loud and aggressive shouting of criticisms became well known in the area as BARRACKING. **WINKT!**

4

Golf

The Scottish origins of golf lie
behind many of its quirky terms –
and it's picked up a good few more
over the centuries since then!

Well, I never knew that . . .
. . . there were ancient links between fishermen
and landowners

Medieval Scottish fishermen walking back along the beaches to their homes would pick up pieces of driftwood and use them to hit pebbles along the ground. If they had time on their hands they sometimes dug a small hole in the sand and competed to knock their stone in first. So was born the game of GOLF and the long and frustrating relationship of golfers with sand!

These early games were often played along the ridges of the sand dunes, and it's from the Old English word for ridge, *hlinc*, that we get the modern word for such courses – LINKS COURSES. During the early 15th century, landowners took up the game and began to play inland, where they chose to recreate the sand areas in small hollows with wooden sides to keep the sand in place. In some sense these sandy areas were there to 'protect' the hole, and as they had wooden sides they were referred to as 'chests' or, using the old Scandinavian

word, BUNKERS. This sense of a walled area to protect something also gives us the other meaning of this word – somewhere to hide when being bombed – and also the terms for a protected area for missiles, a MISSILE BUNKER, and secure storage for fuel, a FUEL BUNKER.

The game proved so popular that in 1457 the Scottish King James II made golf illegal for the masses so that they would practise their archery instead. Unfortunately for Scotland, this law went largely ignored and archers never became a significant part of the Scottish army – unlike their historical enemies the English.

Well, I never knew that . . .
. . . little heads would be sent ahead

Caput is Latin for 'head'; hence the 'head' of a team is a CAPTAIN and a hat worn on the head is often called a CAP. Also, the eldest son in a French family, who was assumed to be the next head of the family, was known as a *caput*. In contrast, the youngest son was called a *capdet*, meaning 'little head'. These youngest sons, who would not inherit their families' fortunes, would offer their services for free to commanders of regiments so that they could begin military careers as officers in the hope of eventually making their own fortunes. Hence officers in training are still known as CADETS. These officers would often be used to carry messages around the regiment, and in Scotland the word was used more widely to describe young men who were available for running errands or carrying small items. Sometimes this included items used in golf; hence the word CADDY. At Oxford University the term was also used to describe boys who ran errands for the upper-class students. The disdain with which these students regarded such 'peasants' led to the term being used in a wider derogatory sense that compared them to scoundrels and petty thieves: CADS.

Pebbles proved difficult to play with and the gentry soon started making their own balls made from feathers pressed into small leather bags. To avoid losing such extravagant items, servants were sent on forward of the play to spot where the ball landed. When he was ready to play, the golfer would shout 'FORWARD!' to get the servants' attention. Over time this was shortened to 'FORE!' Interestingly, for some time caddies were actually known as FORECADDIES.

In the first days of the sport, to get a good first hit the fisherman would often place his stone on a small pile of sand. This was copied by the landowners who took up the game, and small boxes of sand were provided at the start of each hole. In fact, some Scottish courses still have these boxes, although nowadays they are full of soil to replace divots. To the lords, these piles of sand were reminiscent of a the small thatched hovels in which Scottish peasants lived, and so the word for such buildings, *tigh*, was used to describe them.

Over time small wooden pegs were found to be more practical and less messy; but they kept the same name, giving us our word TEE.

By 1848 new and more robust balls were being made, which enabled the introduction of the first metal-headed golf clubs. Then in 1899 the first rubber-based balls were manufactured, to a design that has remained essentially unaltered ever since.

Some players noticed that older balls could be hit further than new balls, and eventually this was connected to the indentations caused by constant use. These marks caused turbulence in the air around the ball, allowing it to pass through the air more easily. Before long such indentations were purposely made in new balls, and so we have the characteristic pattern of DIMPLES on modern golf balls.

It was also discovered that backspin could increase the distance a ball would travel, and hence we have the GROOVES on all modern golf clubs, except those used on the green, where the ball will typically roll along the ground. As these clubs are used to 'put' the ball into the hole they are called PUTTERS and the strokes are called PUTTING.

Like so many sporting associations, golf courses and their social clubs often became an excuse for men to get together and cement their friendship over copious amounts of good wine, and so it is not surprising that the Open Championship Trophy is a very large CLARET JUG! No change there, then . . .

Well, I never knew that . . .
. . . getting the bird in golf is a compliment

Up until the 1950s a rule in golf said that you had to play over or around another player's ball on the putting green even if it was directly in the way of the hole. This was clearly very frustrating and often impossible to achieve. While the rule no longer exists, the word for this situation in golf has survived, now used commonly to describe situations where an apparently easy final step is frustrated at the last: STYMIED.

'Way' is used to describe a ship's movement. When it starts to move, slowly at first, it is UNDER WAY; when it is moving well it is MAKING WAY; and so on. Good or safe conditions at sea are called 'fair': for example, good weather is 'fair weather'. When access to a channel or port is limited, the route that a ship must use to make way safely is called by the word that is also used to describe the 'safe' route to the green in golf: THE FAIRWAY.

The Latin word for 'equal' is used in some sports to represent what a hypothetical good player should be able to achieve. This notional score is then the score that other players should be trying to equal or beat: PAR. A variant of the word 'par' gives us the basis for the word that describes two equal and matching things: PAIR. The process of checking to see if two things are a pair or not gives us the word COMPARE.

Towards the end of the 19th century there was a popular song about a mysterious figure of dread. At this time a golf club reclassified the par rating for its course and also gave the number of strokes that a 'typical' member should be able to get round in – slightly above the par score. However, one of the members sarcastically stated that he didn't know who this 'typical' member was because the score was so very difficult to match. In fact, he must be some invisible member whom no one had ever met – perhaps like the mysterious man in the song. From this has come the term for a score of one stroke over par at a hole: BOGEY, from the song 'The bogey man cometh'.

At the start of the 20th century a golfer called Ab Smith holed a long shot, unexpectedly beating the par by one shot, and said, 'that was a bird of a shot' – from which we get the term BIRDIE, for one under par. Subsequently it was decided that, as two under par was even rarer, this should be named after a rare bird – an EAGLE – and three under par should be named after a bird you would never ever expect even to see on a golf course: ALBATROSS.

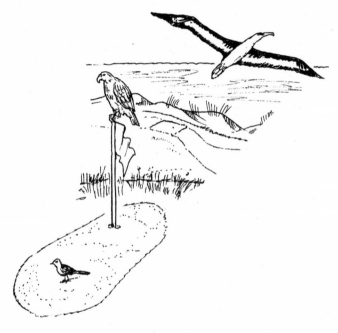

This next expression refers to when two people play a similar stroke from a similar location but one is lucky and the other is not. For example, one may chip onto the green, hit the flag and go in. Another may do likewise but see the ball bounce away from the hole. The phrase is the RUB OF THE GREEN, sometimes shortened to just 'THAT IS THE RUB' or 'THERE'S THE RUB'. **WINKT!**

5

Cricket

Cricket has played such a big part in
our national life that it's not
surprising its terms have come into
common use a long way from
the wicket!

In affectionate Remembrance
OF
ENGLISH CRICKET
WHICH DIED AT THE OVAL
ON
29th AUGUST 1882
Deeply lamented by a large circle of
sorrowing friends and acquaintances
RIP

Well, I never knew that . . .
. . . cricket wasn't always played with a straight bat

As described in appendix II, medieval monks used to play the game of tennis in the courtyards of large monasteries. However, the smaller outlying chapters of monks who managed property away from the central monastery lived in smaller buildings, often without courtyards, and so they couldn't play the game. So over time they established their own version of a bat and ball game that could be played in the fields. As the ball could now be hit a long way instead of bouncing back within a courtyard, there would be players spread around the playing *field* to collect or, even better, catch the ball. Not surprisingly, these players became known as FIELDERS. This game subsequently evolved into one in which the hitter of the ball would run around a series of marked points or bases in order to score a point. Hence in England we call the game ROUNDERS. In America the game evolved again and was named after the places where the hitters could stop en route around the field: BASEBALL.

During the medieval period, shepherds in the south-east of England began to emulate the monks' game of rounders by using stones or matted clumps of wool as balls and their shepherds' crooks as sticks. However, as there were not enough players to have fielders they introduced the use of a tree or tree stump post as a target which the man with the crook would try to defend. As the word for the crook (meaning 'bent') developed into *cryc* it produced the name of the English national game: CRICKET. Incidentally, this is also the source of the phrase for an aching neck as a result of lying down at an awkward angle: a CRICK IN THE NECK. Even though the sport has clearly evolved from these early beginnings, we still retain the link back to the tree *stump* with our term for the wicket: STUMPS.

Bishops often carry a crook in one hand and in the other a staff with a large circular end upon which is a cross. From the Latin *crux* meaning 'cross', this is called a crozier. When early French explorers in North America came across a Native American game using sticks with large circular ends and nets that vaguely resembled the bishops' croziers, they brought the game back to Europe and called it *le jeu de la crosse* or, as we know it, LACROSSE.

Anyway, over time cricket players began to use club-shaped sticks and referred to them using a word derived from 'to beat': BAT. Very soon stones were found to be too dangerous and balls were specially made for the game. Initially they were rolled underarm along the ground, and so we get the French term *boules* or the English BOWLING. During the late 19th century overarm deliveries were allowed, but the old term was retained.

In fact, the terms 'ball', 'bowl' and 'bowling' all belong to a very interesting family of words that go back to an ancient Indo-European word *bhel*, meaning 'swelling' or 'round'.

The idea of someone's rounded tummy gives us the word BELLY. The idea of someone breathing in and making their tummy rounder before exhaling gives us the word BLOW. Combining these words gives us the term for a loud shout from the belly: BELLOW. This in turn gives us the word for a device used to blow air into a fire: BELLOWS. Anything that swells up into a rounded shape becomes BLOATED.

Now, in Latin *bhel* evolved into *bulla* as the Roman word for a bubble. This gave us the term for the bubble-shaped plant we know as a BULB, and subsequently the similarly shaped electric LIGHT BULB. The Roman Catholic Church used the word *bulla* to describe the carved round seal that hung around the neck of the Pope. He would apply this to wax on important official documents to signify his authorization of them: hence the term a PAPAL BULL.

In French, *bulla* evolved into *boule*, which in English then became 'ball'. A very large, inflated ball is called a BALLOON. We also evolved the word to describe a round wooden dish – BOWL – and this spelling was used to describe round wooden balls, BOWLS, and the game in which they were used, BOWLING.

The cricket term 'bowling' therefore actually derives from the much more sedate game of BOWLS. In this game, players bowl against each other in one direction, called an 'end', and then bowl back the other way. Should the jack be hit off the green, then that jack was considered no longer to be 'live'; so we get the phrase A DEAD END. The word 'dead' was also used in the Middle Ages meaning 'completely' or 'totally'. Hence when a pathway comes to a stop, perhaps at a wall, that too is called a dead end. When something was proven to be totally correct it would be DEAD RIGHT.

In cricket, playing without a big backswing and with an upright bat to protect the stumps is considered cautious, safe and gentlemanly, and usually plays the ball straight back to where it came from; hence our phrase meaning to conduct oneself in a straightforward and courteous manner: PLAYING WITH A STRAIGHT BAT.

While only 11 men play in a cricket team, there is always a reserve in case of injury. However, this person rarely actually plays, and so the position has became associated with disappointment and failing to achieve, even though the man holding it could easily have made something of it if only he had had the opportunity: TWELFTH MAN.

Well, I never knew that . . .
. . . umpires were aristocratic equals

Cricket has always been a gentleman's game in which honour and fair play are deemed important; hence a phrase meaning *not* gentlemanly: 'THAT'S NOT CRICKET.'

An early English word derived from the Latin *par*, meaning 'equal', has given us the word for someone who is considered equal in status: a PEER. This assessment of who was and who was not one's equal was especially important for lords, who would use it when referring to their fellow nobles to bring clarity to the pecking order of feudal society. Hence, over time, the word 'peer' gained the extra specific meaning of a LORD OF THE REALM.

In France a concept had developed that if you need unbiased arbitration between two peers, someone who is above their level (and is therefore not a peer) should be involved. Using two words, *non* (meaning 'not') and *pair* (meaning 'peer'), the French created a new word meaning just that: *nonpair*. This evolved into *nompair* and then *numpere*. It came to Britain as *a numpire*. However, people misheard or misunderstood the phrase and over time it became – an UMPIRE.

In the 19th century a rule was passed that still applies to cricket stating that a fielder cannot catch a batsman out by using his *hat*! Just imagine the situation that must have resulted in that rule being added!

There used to be a tradition that if a bowler got three batsmen out with three consecutive balls he would be presented with a hat of honour by his club to commemorate his good play. He was then entitled to walk around the crowd and collect money or gifts given by the crowd to show their admiration. This gives us the phrase HAT TRICK.

A lesser-known cricketing term is the phrase for bowling two batsmen out with just two consecutive balls. The term is actually used more widely than in cricket and derives from the Latin word for arms, *bracchia*. The word evolved into the old French word *brace*, and this came to be applied to the arm pieces of armour. As there were two of these in each set of armour, the word then became associated with the number two. Hence we get a brace of ducks, a brace of pheasants and in cricket, when two wickets fall to two consecutive balls, a BRACE OF BATSMEN! Incidentally, from using one's arms to hug another person we get the term EMBRACE, and from here the idea of providing support gives us the meaning of the word for an item of clothing, as in BELT AND BRACES, and even the braces used to reposition someone's front teeth – a TEETH BRACE.

If a cricketer partners another player who does exceptionally well he may get some credit for being part of the partnership. However, it is the player who did the hitting himself who will rightfully claim the accolade – having done it all OFF HIS OWN BAT.

In 1797 Thomas Lord built a sports ground in what is now Dorset Square, London. However, he had to move it twice, and each time he took the turf with him. It is now based in St John's Wood and is better known as LORD'S CRICKET GROUND. This is the headquarters of the MCC or, in full, the MARYLEBONE CRICKET CLUB.

At the end of a game of cricket the stumps need to be drawn out of the ground and stored for the next game. This gives us a phrase we use nowadays to mean that something has finished: DRAWING STUMPS or simply 'STUMPS'.

When at war with an enemy there is a tendency to denigrate anything associated with that country. An example comes from the Napoleonic wars, where this gentleman's sport was reduced down to a simpler version for children and labelled as coming from France: FRENCH CRICKET.

Well, I never knew that . . .

. . . the most important stumps are now only four inches high

In 1882 the Australian cricket team decisively beat England at the Oval. A joke obituary was written by Reginald Brooks in the *Sporting Times*:

'In affectionate Remembrance of English Cricket which died at the Oval on 29th August 1882, deeply lamented by a large circle of sorrowing friends and acquaintances. RIP. NB The body will be cremated and the ashes taken to Australia.'

Subsequently, a bail from a set of cricket stumps was burnt and the ashes were placed in a small urn, just four inches high, and labelled THE ASHES. Ever since, the ownership of these ashes has been fiercely contested between England and Australia in what are called the Ashes test matches.

In 1933 England won the Ashes, but only by introducing a controversial style of bowling where the line of the ball was directed at the batsman's body, causing apprehension, frequent ducking and dodging, and even occasional injury. While successful, it was considered ungentlemanly and resulted in the rules of cricket being changed. The approach was known as BODYLINE BOWLING.

A bowler will often try to lull a batsman into a false sense of security by delivering several slow balls and then suddenly sending down an extremely hard and fast ball by pulling his arm downwards very rapidly. Hence we get the phrase to mean trying on a trick: PULLING A FAST ONE.

Ideally a batsman will be ready for a ball and step towards it to play his stroke. However, if he is caught unprepared or off balance, he may have to sway backwards to defend against a fast ball – in which case, he is CAUGHT ON THE BACK FOOT.

The cricket pitch has a rope around it that defines the edge or 'boundary'. If the batsman hits a ball very skilfully and very hard, it may travel over this rope and not hit the ground until it gets the other side, scoring six runs. Such achievement is sure to get applause from the crowd and be a blow to the bowler; so it gives us a phrase for something or someone hit very hard: KNOCKED FOR SIX.

Well, I never knew that . . .
. . . if you're on a sticky wicket you might well play for time

When a cricket pitch is being lightly rained upon, or is drying out in the sun after a brief shower, it can be difficult for a batsman to assess how the ball will bounce – whether it will sink into the mud and have a deadened bounce, or not. This is very difficult for the batsmen, giving rise to a phrase meaning tricky conditions: A STICKY WICKET.

Occasionally a batsman starts as one of the first two and survives the whole innings without being out, at which point he walks off proudly with his bat. This has given us the phrase meaning that someone has outlasted his opponents and has fully completed his (or her) commitments: TO CARRY ONE'S BAT.

In cricket, if the batting side is not all out at the end of a match – even if one side is far ahead of the other in the number of runs scored – then the result is a DRAW. This rule means that if a side is losing and it is coming to the end of the day, instead of trying to score as many runs as possible they may decide to play defensively just to survive until time runs out. A related phrase is now used more widely, especially in football where one team is ahead and would rather waste time and play defensively than try to score another goal and in so doing risk the other side counter-attacking and scoring an equalizer: PLAYING FOR TIME.

Incidentally, if both sides in a cricket match are all out with the same score, the result is called a TIE. This word comes from the old English word *teag*, meaning 'rope'. Joining two ropes together became tieing or TYING them together. Hence two teams whose scores could not be separated were said to be TIED. Also, the idea of a cravat being knotted around a man's neck gives us a NECKTIE, usually shortened to simply TIE. In the same way, a cottage that goes with a job on the landowner's estate is a TIED COTTAGE and a pub that is owned by a brewery and so must sell its beer is a TIED PUB. **WINKT!**

6

Hunting, Shooting and Fishing

You might be surprised how many phrases we use every day had bloodthirsty origins in the sports that were popular in less sensitive times.

Well, I never knew that . . .
. . . venison is a deer that's out of breath

The Norman nobles loved hunting and William the Conqueror established several areas in which animals were kept for the chase. These areas were named using the old French word for enclosure, *parc,* itself derived from the Latin *parricus;* we know them as PARKS (from which, of course, we also get the term for an enclosed space for cars: CAR PARK).

He also established areas of woodland 'outside' parks as his own hunting domains. Using the words *foresti,* meaning 'outside' (from which we also get the term for someone from outside your home territory: FOREIGN), and *sylva,* meaning a wood, these were called *foresti sylva* – literally, 'outside woods'. The *sylva* element was soon dropped, leaving 'forest', as in the case of the newly created area on the south coast of England: THE NEW FOREST.

Dheus was an old Indo-European word meaning breath, and was initially applied to anything that breathed. However, it soon came to be applied to the Normans' favourite animal to hunt, which would be chased until it became breathless and slowed down enough to be speared. Hence our word for this animal: DEER. Male deer are very majestic and were named after the old English generic word for any male at the height of his masculinity, *stagga,* giving us our word STAG and, of course, the term for a group of men's celebrations before one of them gets married: a STAG NIGHT. The Latin word for 'to hunt' was *venari,* and again, as deer was the favoured animal for nobles to hunt, before long deer meat was referred to as VENISON.

Once an animal was caught it would be gutted to make it lighter to carry and the hunting dogs would be allowed to eat the innards as a reward. The heart was usually deep red, being full of oxygenated blood from all the running, as so dogs would often go for that first; and so the reward was called *coree* from *cor,* the word for 'heart'. The skin would also be removed before cooking; this too would be given to the dogs, and the combination of *coree* and the French word for animal skin, *cuir,* led to the pelt being called *cuirée.* Eventually this word was applied to the animal while it was being chased, and because it sounded like an existing English word for mining it became misspelt as QUARRY – which has nothing, incidentally, to do with the same word for an opencast mine.

Hunting has been associated with royalty for centuries, which is why most coats in British hunts are coloured RED (from the royal standard of a red background with golden lions), whereas in France the colour for hunting is BLUE (from the French royal standard of a blue background with yellow *fleurs-de-lis*).

When in constant use in a range of weather conditions the bright red can fade slightly, and so the jackets are referred to as 'pinks'. In fact, this term is now used even when they are brand new. As a day's hunting is an opportunity to have fun and forget about any pressures of life, we have a phrase for people who are happy: IN THE PINK!

When hounds have lost the scent and the huntsman calls them back, he uses a command that has become common in

general speech, meaning to return to a previous point in a discussion or topic: TO HARK BACK.

When hunting with dogs, if a hunted animal enters property where a hunt is not authorized to go or where the hounds lose the scent of their prey, the huntsman needs to get them out and back under control. Hence the phrase CALL THE DOGS OFF.

Well, I never knew that . . .

. . . the game's up if you're caught missing a three-line whip

In a game hunt there would often be two phases. The first would involve a large number of unarmed beaters banging sticks or drums and making a noise to move the intended prey through the undergrowth without confronting it. From this we get the phrase referring to a cautious and indirect approach: BEATING ABOUT THE BUSH. Then, having been found, the game suddenly stands up and is flushed out of its hiding place. This would be followed by the climax of the hunt, which would involve either a quick chase to the death or the shooting of the prey. Hence when someone or something is flushed out of hiding we say THE GAME IS UP.

In the 19th century some mounted fox hunters were having no luck catching a fox, and so they decided to have a race across the fields, hedges and streams to a church spire that they could just see in the distance. From this we get the name of a horse race now run across purpose-built fences and water jumps: a STEEPLECHASE.

Incredibly, due to excessive hunting and over-zealous gamekeepers, there was a shortage of foxes for hunting in southern England during the early 19th century, and so French foxes were imported and sold at London's Leadenhall market. These foxes would be transported in bags, along with other illicit goods such as French brandy. Hence the phrase now usually associated with someone involved in underhand dealing in money gained through crime and extortion: a BAGMAN.

One person with an important role in fox hunting is the horseman who keeps the hounds together by using a hunting

97

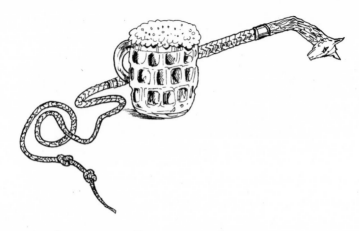

horn and occasionally a knotted rope or whip, and is consequently called the WHIPPER-IN. By analogy, the parliamentarian who keeps Members of Parliament of his or her party in order is called a PARTY WHIP. Before an important division where every vote is crucial the party whip will send a note to each MP underlined a number of times to show the level of importance. The most important is a THREE-LINE WHIP.

Well, I never knew that . . .
. . . if you're in the mess when there's a whip round,
you're fair game

Because many army officers used to be from the country gentry and keen fox hunters, if they needed to collect money in the officers' mess for drinks they would nominate an officer as the 'whipper-in' to go around and collect it. This was called a WHIP ROUND.

Ultimately derived from the Latin word *capere* meaning to take (from which we get the word CAPTURE), the Old English word *cacchen* developed, meaning to hunt. From here we get the words for the process of hunting, a CHASE, and actually getting hold of the prey so that it can be captured or killed, CATCH. The application of the word to fishing gave the word a slightly more passive meaning, as in CATCHING A FISH, and eventually also phrases such as CATCHING A BALL or CATCHING A COLD.

In France, the word *chasseur*, which means 'hunter', has been used to describe light infantrymen (often ex-hunters) who operate in a skirmishing and informal manner. In Germany the directly equivalent word is JAEGER.

Hunting seasons are clearly defined, with fixed starting and ending dates between which it is legitimate to hunt certain game animals. Outside these dates they cannot be hunted. Inside the dates they are considered to be FAIR GAME.

Possums live in trees and would usually be hunted at night with specially trained dogs that tracked them down by smell. There would be a lot of barking to try to scare the possums into staying put until the hunters came to shoot them, but in the noise, darkness and general confusion sometimes the hunter would turn up and find there was no possum in the tree. Then the frustrated hunter would say that his dogs had been BARKING UP THE WRONG TREE.

Interestingly, turkeys do not come from Turkey as you may expect, but rather from NORTH AMERICA. You see, around 1600 a new type of fowl, somewhat like a chicken, was imported for the first time from Turkey. It became known as the turkey fowl. Many years later similar birds were imported from Guinea on the west coast of Africa; to distinguish them from the turkey fowl, these were called GUINEA FOWL. Another similar bird was then discovered in America. This turned out to be a slightly different and larger breed, and it helped breeders to realize that the original turkey fowl and guinea fowl were in fact one and the same breed. However, guinea fowl by now commanded a premium price in English restaurants, and so suppliers chose to apply this name to the birds from Turkey as well. This allowed the old term to be applied to the new bird from America – TURKEY FOWL – even though it had no connection with the country at all! The word fowl was soon dropped, giving us our word TURKEY.

The large, ungainly turkeys from America were rather stupid and relatively easy to track down and kill, and so gave us another term for a task that is easy to perform: a TURKEY SHOOT. The combination of appearing stupid and dying as a result of it also gives us the term for someone who does stupid things with potentially risky outcomes: A TURKEY.

Well, I never knew that . . .
. . . if you don't talk turkey you might ruin the whole
shooting match

Early US settlers followed the native American hunting habits of tracking down wild turkeys and then making gobbling sounds to encourage the birds to come closer so they could get an easy shot. This skill enabled the hunt to be carried out faster and more efficiently, and gave us a phrase that still means getting the job done well: TALKING TURKEY.

When shooting game birds the firing can be almost continuous, with loaders constantly providing loaded guns for those taking part in the shoot. The honours go to the person who shoots most birds. The event will often take the best part of a day and will stop only when all the ammunition has been used up, or when there are no more birds to shoot. Hence the phrase meaning holding nothing back: THE WHOLE SHOOT or THE WHOLE SHOOTING MATCH.

In medieval archery contests, competitors would end up shooting at targets that were further and further away, requiring them to arc their arrows *up* into the air. Eventually only one archer would be able to hit the target and he would be declared the winner. The final shot was given the name that subsequently came to mean any final outcome: the UPSHOT!

Well, I never knew that . . .
. . . Nelson died in the driving seat

Cockfighting used to be a very popular sport across Europe and was strongly associated with gambling. Pits were often dug to provide places for all kinds of blood sports, such as badger baiting; however, cockfighting was by far the most common and so the pits became known as COCKPITS. The rooms on board galleons where wounded sailors were taken for surgery during sea battles would always be bloody and messy places and in fact were often painted red to hide the copious amounts of blood. Due to the link with severe injuries and death, as in cockfighting, these 'surgeries' were also called COCKPITS. When Nelson was shot at the Battle of Trafalgar in

1805 he was taken to HMS *Victory*'s cockpit where he eventually died. Incidentally, the area where the steersman stands in a modern yacht is also called a cockpit, although this is not because of what happens there but because of its shape resembling the original pits in the ground. By the same analogy, the place where the driver sits in a Formula One racing car and where a pilot sits in an aeroplane is also called a COCKPIT – though the latter still echoes the original use, being based upon the early First World War biplanes with a single seat into which the pilot would climb, ready for a fight to the death with an opponent.

When bets had been placed on a cockfight and the birds were ready, they would simply be thrown into the *pit* and made to fight until one died. This is why we say that opponents in any sort of contest are PITTED AGAINST EACH OTHER. King Henry VIII loved cockfighting and especially liked the variant when several cocks were thrown in at one time and left to fight until only one was left alive. This royal connection gives us a phrase which is still used to describe multi-person boxing matches in the USA where the winner is literally the last man

standing: a BATTLE ROYAL. The same term is now also used more widely to describe any vicious, prolonged and exciting contest.

Cockerels have a naturally occurring sharp claw-type prong at the back of each leg and used these, together with their sharp beaks, to cause serious wounds to their opponents. They could be augmented by strapping hollow, very sharp metal blades to the legs over the prongs to provide even more lethal weapons. These were considered to resemble the spurs that horse riders wore to urge on their horses, and so were also called SPURS. The popularity of this practice, and indeed the sport as a whole, explains the fairly common road names in England COCKSPUR ROAD and COCKPIT STREET.

Well, I never knew that . . .
. . . the sharpest thing in sparring is a cutting remark

Training these birds to fight was important to make them efficient killing machines, but clearly the owners would not want them injured unless they were fighting for real money. So for training fights they would remove the metal spurs and possibly even wrap the prongs in cloth. From the Latin word *pare*, meaning 'to make ready', the word *ex-pare* developed, and then evolved into *espare*. This new word subsequently transferred to boxing, where in training boxers practise manoeuvring around the ring but will not land heavy punches with their full weight behind them. Over time this word became SPARRING. This term has subsequently been applied to debates, especially where both sides respect each other but dispute the logic of each other's argument, giving us the term VERBAL SPARRING.

Incidentally, *pare* also gives us the word for making ready in advance – PREPARE – and the word for being ready for an attacking stroke with a sword and so being able to deflect it – PARRY.

Several different types of birds were especially bred for cockfighting. One breed in particular was considered very brave, aggressive and courageous, even against bigger birds. Birds of this breed had very dark plumage, and so many people would be reluctant to bid on a bird that had many white feathers, as this showed it was not a pure-bred fighting cock and therefore might not be a very good fighter. This led to an association of white feathers with weakness or even cowardice, so that during the First World War men who avoided being called up to go and fight in the trenches would often receive THREE WHITE FEATHERS through their letterbox. **WINKT!**

7

Horse Racing

Horse racing has long been known
as 'the Sport of Kings' – but has
given us some colourful language
from right across the
social spectrum!

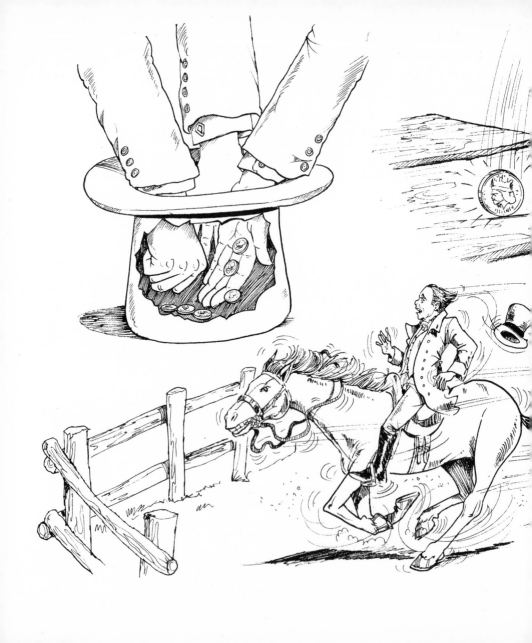

Well, I never knew that . . .
. . . if you put your hand in the cap you may get mud
in your eye

Horses' hooves throw up mud or dust in the face of anyone behind them. From this has developed a competitive toast in which you state you will be ahead of your opponents and that they will suffer the indignity of being not only beaten but also physically splattered as well: 'HERE'S MUD IN YOUR EYE!'

If a horse race is exciting and the horse you bet on ran very fast and put full effort in, you may say that, even though eventually it didn't win and so you lost your bet, 'IT GAVE ME A GOOD RUN FOR MY MONEY'.

An old form of barter involved two people wishing to trade and a neutral third party. A forfeit would be set and all three put the agreed number of 'forfeit' coins into their hands and then place their closed fists into a central large cap. The third person would then decide if one side should provide money in addition to the item being swapped to make the exchange fair. Each trader then decided if he wished to go ahead on that basis or not. If he did, he left the forfeit in the cap and removed his hand. If not, he took his forfeit out. If all parties left their forfeits in the hat, then the deal went ahead. If the deal did go ahead, the third party took the forfeits. If the deal did not go through and one person had left his money in,

he took that money back and the umpire's forfeit as well. This encouraged the third party to create a deal acceptable to both sides. This 'game' was called HAND IN THE CAP. This idea of a third party deciding what was fair was applied to horse racing in the form of giving light

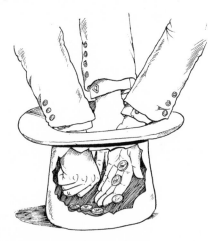

jockeys extra weight to carry to even out the horses' chances. This process of assessing the weights was called HANDI-CAPPING, and a horse race where the weights are varied in this way came to be known as a HANDICAP. Clearly this idea of handicapping has subsequently been used much more widely.

In the early 20th century two aligned wires were introduced on opposite sides of the course at the finishing line for many horse races. This enabled a steward to see very clearly which horse had crossed the finishing line first. When two horses were neck and neck and the victory could only be decided by the steward at the finishing line it was described as going DOWN TO THE WIRE.

Well, I never knew that . . .
. . . a horse with the bit between its teeth may well get
out of hand

When a jockey is enjoying a large lead at the end of a race, he can afford to let the horse coast in without riding him hard. In practice this means allowing his arms and hands to drop and let the reins hang relatively loose; hence the phrase for an easy victory, WINNING HANDS DOWN. The piece of metal that sits in the horse's mouth, attached to the reins, and helps a rider control a horse is named after the old Saxon word for biting, *bita*, giving us BIT. If a horse is very keen to gallop off it is often constrained by the rider pulling on the reins, which in turn pulls the bit tighter. The horse will try to move the bit in its mouth to gain control, so we say of someone who is eager to escape restraint and get on with something that they are CHAMPING AT THE BIT. If the horse succeeds in biting on the bit, the rider loses control and the horse can charge away; it has GOT THE BIT BETWEEN ITS TEETH. If the rider is holding the horse back by pulling on the reins and then releases them, this allows the horse to push its head forward and gallop off at top

117

speed, and so is called GIVING THE HORSE ITS HEAD. The reins are also used to direct the horse, and if the horse is allowed to some extent to choose the direction of travel, it is called GIVING THE HORSE FREE REIN. If the horse suddenly pulls away and the rider loses hold of the reins, then the situation has literally got OUT OF HAND.

The people who run the gambling at racecourses keep records of who has placed what bets and how much money they are making in special books. Hence they are called BOOKMAKERS or BOOKIES. Bookies always like as many horses in a race as possible, because this means that more people will bet, and that there are more runners who will not win. Hence if a horse arrives at the last minute and is included in a race its name is added to 'the book' and is good news for the bookie – A TURN UP FOR THE BOOKS.

If someone claimed to have made a bet but it was not recorded, the bookie would say something that nowadays means a different understanding of a situation: 'NOT IN MY BOOK'.

Well, I never knew that . . .
. . . a dead ringer could be a very live prospect

American bookmakers used to list horses vertically on their display boards, and then the finishing positions from left to right. If a gambler bet on a horse coming in the first three places it was called betting ACROSS THE BOARD. The phrase is now used more widely to mean covering a wide range of people or circumstances. A horse that comes first, second or third has its name written up or 'placed' on the winners' board, hence the bookies' term PLACED. The term for a horse that also ran in the race but did not get placed is now used more widely for someone who is not a winner at anything: an ALSO RAN.

Early counterfeit coins could be detected by dropping them on to a hard surface and listening very carefully. Fake coins, with different metal content from genuine ones, did not make the correct ringing sound. Hence our phrase 'THAT DOESN'T RING TRUE'. Subsequently these coins were called 'ringers'. In horse racing, deviously replacing one horse with another (either much better or much worse than the original, to the benefit of those in on the trick) before a race was also called RINGING and the horse was called a RINGER. In case anyone had

seen the original horse beforehand, the ringer would need to look similar, and if it was very well known it would need to be virtually identical. Hence, using the old word for exact, 'dead' (as in 'dead centre'), we get the phrase meaning an almost exact copy: DEAD RINGER. This term is now used more widely, especially for actors who impersonate celebrities.

Keeping a goat as companion for a horse is a well-known way of calming it down – especially a highly strung thoroughbred. In fact, as horse racing became increasingly popular during the 18th and 19th centuries these goats would sometimes be stolen just before a race to unnerve a potential winner. Hence the phrase we use meaning to have caused serious annoyance or anxiety: HE HAS GOT MY GOAT.

At around the same time, it became common practice for a likely winner to be bribed to lose a race unexpectedly and hence allow unscrupulous gamblers to trick the bookies and win at very long odds. This was called TRICKING. Sometimes, though, a rider would take the bribe and still go on and win. This was called DOUBLE TRICKING.

Before buying a horse it is a good idea to test it out by riding it in all four of its paces: walk, trot, canter and gallop. Thus when we give any unfamiliar machine or new invention a thorough trial we say we are PUTTING IT THROUGH ITS PACES.

Well, I never knew that . . .
. . . a crooked bishop might have looked a gift horse
in the mouth

Two other phrases have evolved from the habit of checking a horse before purchase by the appearance of its mouth, which can be a good indication of age and overall health. The first refers to the fact that a horse's gums recede as it get older, and therefore the amount of tooth that is visible is a good indication of its age; so an animal or person who is getting old is a bit LONG IN THE TOOTH. One unscrupulous clergyman was discovered to have filed down the teeth of older horses to make them appear younger so that he could sell them at a higher price. Ever since, such deceit has been called BISHOPING. The second phrase is often used differently from how it was originally intended. It refers to the discourteous behaviour of publicly assessing the worth and quality of a gift before accepting it, instead of graciously accepting the gift and then examining it in private: LOOKING A GIFT HORSE IN THE MOUTH.

Many words based on Indo-European based sources evolved with different spellings through the French and Germanic languages. This often involves a Germanic 'g' becoming a 'w' in French. Examples are 'guardian' and 'warden', and their derivatives 'guard' and 'ward' and 'guarantee' and 'warranty'. The same thing happened with the word for how a horse runs, 'gallop', and a less often used word for the same thing, 'wallup'. Over time, the latter became associated with how you made a horse gallop, hence the term for hitting: WALLOP.

In 1779 an English aristocrat initiated a horse race for three-year-old fillies called the Oaks. The following year he discussed another race, this time for three-year-old colts, with his friend Sir Charles Bunbury. They tossed a coin to see which one of them the race would be named after. The race became a very popular event in which the competition became very fierce, to the point where the name of the race began to be used in other sports where there was intense rivalry: it was DERBY, from the Earl of Derby who won the toss. In fact, using coins in this way became a very popular way of deciding who should be the winner where there was no obvious logic as a basis for the decision. If someone wanted to show that, in fact, it was not that important for him to win or not, he would simply let the other person win without even using the coin – NOT GIVING A TOSS.

Once a coin has been tossed and has landed and the outcome is known, there is no point in further continuing the debate over who has won: so you DON'T ARGUE THE TOSS.

In medieval times there was a horse race that took place in two parts. The first part was a straight race to decide who would lead the second part. The second part involved one rider emulating a goose trying to evade capture from the other riders by riding around in random directions. This race was called A WILD GOOSE CHASE.   **WINKT!**

8

Other Sports

From swordplay to swimming, from
badminton to bicycling, all our
favourite sports have something new
to tell us about our language.

Well, I never knew that . . .

. . . if you want to call the shots, you'll need a quick riposte

Several English words have been adopted from the sport of fencing. One is the French word for a blocking deflection, which comes from the Latin word *pare*, 'to make ready'. This word is now used in a much wider sense: PARRY. Another is the French word for a swordsman's counter-attack, nowadays meaning a swift retort: RIPOSTE.

The fencing foil has a tapering blade. The thickest and strongest part gives us the term for a person's natural strength: FORTE (from *fort*, French for 'strong', from which we also get the word for a strong defensive position: FORTRESS or simply FORT; and the word for wine that has been strengthened with brandy, such as port: FORTIFIED WINE). The bendy part of a foil is relatively 'feeble', and so we get the term for someone's weakness: FOIBLE ('foil' and 'feeble' combined).

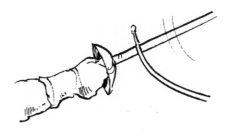

Another fencing term, used when one swordsman hits or touches his opponent in a scoring area, is nowadays used in a debate when one person scores a rapid and particularly good 'hit' in response to his opponent's argument: TOUCHÉ (from the French for 'touched').

In the game of pool you must not hit the number eight ball until you have pocketed your other balls. If this ball blocks the cue ball then you are in a difficult situation: BEHIND THE EIGHT BALL.

In pool, whoever is about to play can choose which ball they will try to pocket next, giving us the phrase for being in control and able to choose a direction: CALLING THE SHOTS.

Well, I never knew that . . .
. . . once you've taken the strain you need to keep it up

When a Frenchman invented a two-wheeled machine that the user sat upon and pushed along with his feet they called it 'fast foot': *vélocipede* or *vélo* for short. Very quickly a magazine was created for enthusiasts called *Le Vélo*. In 1903 the French sports magazine *L'Auto* created what was originally a publicity stunt to beat its competitor *Le Vélo*. The stunt has turned into an annual event that is now one of the most widely watched sporting events in the world: LE TOUR DE FRANCE. In 1931 another publicity stunt was introduced: the awarding of a prize to the lead rider at the end of each day, in the form of a garment in the same bright colour as the pages of *L'Auto* magazine: THE YELLOW JERSEY.

The Greek word *kuklos* meaning 'round' gives us the words 'circle' and 'cycle', from which we call such a machine with two (*bi*) wheels a BICYCLE.

In a tug of war, just before both sides fully exert themselves, an instruction is given to lean back and pull gently. This phrase is now commonplace in preparation for any physical effort: TAKE THE STRAIN.

The Indian game of Poona was brought back to England by officers in the mid-19th century. It was very popular with the

Duke of Beaufort, who championed it in the UK, and so it was named after his family seat in Gloucestershire: BADMINTON.

Scytle is an old English word for an arrow or other fast-moving missile. This is the root of the word used in the industrial revolution to describe a very fast-moving piece of machinery in a cotton loom that flicked from one side to another: the SHUTTLE. By analogy, more recently a fast-moving train, tram or bus that travels backwards and forwards between two locations is also called a SHUTTLE. The same word also describes the projectile used in a racquet game whose

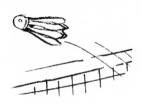

poor aerodynamics mean that it has to be hit upwards. Combined with 'cock', an old word meaning 'upwards', as in 'cocking' a gun, it gives us SHUTTLECOCK.

Beginners at badminton often have to be reminded to strike the shuttlecock upwards in order to do well and keep a rally going: hence the phrase KEEP IT UP.

Well, I never knew that . . .
. . . the royal yacht goes a long way further back
than Britannia

Bios is Greek for life, and *aero* is Greek for air – and so we have the word for exercise that helps life by getting plenty of oxygen into the body: AEROBICS.

The old English *lepen* (to jump) gives us the closely related word LEAP. With 'inter', meaning 'between', it also gives us the idea of someone jumping into a situation where they should not be: INTERLOPER.

For whistles to produce their shrill sound they need a clean flow of air and in some designs a freely rotating ball. This can be impeded by dirt with a dramatic effect upon the tone. Hence the expression AS CLEAN AS A WHISTLE.

Jagd was Old German for 'hunt'. A variant of this word was used to describe woodsmen, and then lightly equipped, fast-moving soldiers: JAEGER. The word was then applied to a very fast style of sailing ship designed to chase the pirates who were conducting hit-and-run attacks on merchantmen along the German and Dutch coast. These were called *jagdschips*, and eventually caught the attention of the Dutch aristocracy who used such ships for pleasure. This was during the period of Charles II's exile in the Netherlands, and when he was restored to the throne in England the Dutch people gave him one of these ships as a gift. He had another built for his brother the Duke of York, whom he then raced up and down the Thames to the North Sea. This made it a 'must have' accessory for the British aristocracy, who then had their own versions made. The name of these ships was adapted for the English tongue, and they became known as YACHTS.

If a diver goes very deep and then surfaces too rapidly the nitrogen in his blood can form bubbles. This causes excruciating pain, which can be so bad that the diver may well be bent double in agony; hence this potentially fatal condition is called THE BENDS.

Underwater breathing apparatus has evolved over many decades. A particular breakthrough was made by Jacques Cousteau in the mid-20th century with the invention of what he called the *Self-Contained Underwater Breathing Apparatus,* enabling the activity we know as SCUBA-DIVING.

Well, I never knew that . . .
. . . one cox didn't pull his weight when the race had started

In the late 19th century a competitive rower identified that in the four-man boat the steering role of the cox could be undertaken by the rearmost rower controlling it with his feet. The rules, however, required that a cox be in the boat at the start of the race. So as soon as the race started, the cox jumped over the side and the remaining four oarsmen easily won the race as they were carrying much less weight than their competitors! Hence the creation of a new type of boat race that takes place in parallel to the standard four-man race: THE COXLESS FOUR.

Rowing requires everyone on board to row together and to use their muscles and whole bodyweight to maximize speed; hence the phrase TO PULL YOUR WEIGHT.

An Italian word, *rigatto*, meaning 'contention', was used in medieval days to describe races in Venice between the various gondola owners. The word has now evolved to mean water-based races in general, with one of the most famous being held at Henley upon Thames each June: REGATTA. In medieval Venice the gondola owners became very extravagant in decorating their gondolas to compete with one another for the richest passengers. Eventually this display reached ludicrous levels with the use of gold leaf and silver adornments, and the doge (duke) declared that all gondolas would have to be painted PLAIN BLACK all over – a rule that still applies to this day.

Well, I never knew that . . .
. . . the butterfly could beat the strongest swimmers

The original rules for the breast stroke stipulated simply that both arms should be moved forward simultaneously. However, this led to the creation of a new stroke that met the rules but came to dominate the event because it was so effective – for those who could do it. This new stroke was named after a creature that appeared to move in a similar way: THE BUTTERFLY STROKE. In response, an additional rule was introduced for the breast stroke event that was designed to prevent the new stroke being used: HANDS CANNOT BREAK THE SURFACE OF THE WATER. The butterfly stroke now has its own event.

A group of freshwater fish that happened to be swimming together used to be called a 'swim'. This would clearly be an ideal place for a fisherman to cast his line, giving us a phrase meaning taking advantage of a good situation IN THE SWIM.

Beita is an old Viking word meaning 'to bite'. This gives us not only our word 'bite' but also the name of a tasty morsel designed to make a fish or other animal come close enough to be caught: BAIT.

The Greek word *anklos* meaning 'bent' gives us the words for the part of a leg that allows the foot to bend, ANKLE, and a bend in a straight line, an ANGLE. This word was also used to

describe a bent piece of metal used to catch fish, and so such fishermen were called ANGLERS. Incidentally, a Germanic tribe that lived on a piece of land that was roughly the shape of a fish hook were known as the Angles, from which ultimately we get the name ENGLAND.

Well, I never knew that . . .
. . . ninepence is nothing to do with counting your change

A game developed where pieces of wood were stood on end and another piece of wood was thrown at them with the aim of knocking them all over. As all of the pieces of wood were the same they were collectively referred using the old word for a projectile, *scytle*. Hence we get the name of the game: SKITTLES. Subsequently the thrown piece of wood has been replaced by a ball.

Skittles, in one form or another, has been a popular game for many centuries. An early form involved nine skittles set up in a square or diamond shape. It was important that the ninepins were set up in exactly the right position before the

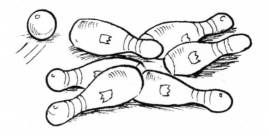

game could begin: hence the phrase AS RIGHT AS NINEPINS or, in a slightly corrupted form, AS RIGHT AS NINEPENCE, meaning that everything is ready to go. The objective of the game was to knock all the skittles over with just one ball (with each falling skittle knocking over one or more of the other skittles). This chain reaction gives us the phrase GOING DOWN LIKE NINEPINS. If after two attempts a player had just three pins left standing in a triangular pattern he could still win the game. This was considered to look like the shape of a tricorn hat (a wide-brimmed hat with the brim folded or 'cocked' up in three places). The phrase to describe this outcome was 'TO HAVE BEEN KNOCKED INTO A COCKED HAT'. In the 18th and 19th centuries the game became a popular vehicle for gambling and as a result was banned in London and major cities

across America. To get round the legislation a bowling-alley proprietor in the United States introduced a slight change – the inclusion of another skittle or pin – and hence created the modern version: TEN-PIN BOWLING. At this stage it became more difficult to knock all the pins over, and if someone did achieve it they would be BOWLED OVER with their success.

In ten-pin bowling the ideal shot is to hit the front pin in a particular way so that all the other pins fall over. This front pin has been given a nickname reflecting its importance, which is now used more widely to mean someone who is crucial in a situation, with the implication that if that person fails, so will everyone else: KINGPIN.

Because great precision is needed to *strike* the kingpin in this way, knocking all ten pins over with the first ball is still called a STRIKE.

One old variation of skittles, called duckpins, involved throwing balls at a line of skittles that were supposed to represent ducks. After playing one game the next player would set up their duckpins. Hence the phrase meaning getting everything organized and ready: GET YOUR DUCKS IN A ROW.

Well, I never knew that . . .
. . . a famous London road is named after a 'balls up'!

A game which originated in Italy was called *pallo a maglio* (ball to mallet). It became very popular with the gentry of France where the game was called *paille mall*. The game was then taken to Scotland in the 16th century as a result of the very close links between France and Scotland that were forged through their mutual dislike of England. It was then introduced to England by the Scottish line of Stuart kings.

In 1660 King Charles built an area specifically for playing this game in St James's Park, London, and so many onlookers went there to watch the King play the game that the road that went past it adopted the name of the game: PALL MALL.

In fact, this whole area became very popular and fashionable for walking, and the words became strongly associated with walking. Soon afterwards another road was built nearby called simply THE MALL. As the onlookers would then move on to the nearby shops the road name became associated with relaxed and convenient shopping. From this we get the late 20th-century dedicated shopping areas: MALLS.

The rules of pall mall enabled a skilful player who shot his ball through hoops and hit other balls in the right order to take many shots in one turn, and thus progress around the playing area extremely quickly. From this aggressive winning strategy we get the phrase for an aggressive and fast-moving fight: PELL MELL. Nelson said to his captains just before Trafalgar that the battle would be a 'pell mell'. In pell mell the mallets had one end (and sometimes both ends) of the mallet cut at an angle to be able to raise the ball into the air when struck to go through a metal ring suspended a short distance off the ground. In the 19th century another version of the game pall mall evolved, played with a different-shaped mallet that some people thought resembled a giant crochet hook. It is called CROQUET. **WINKT!**

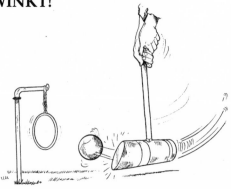

9

Cards and Gambling

People have gambled for as long as they have had a hope of winning and anything to lose – and, life being a risky business, many of the gambler's turns of phrase have worked their way into our everyday language.

Well, I never knew that . . .
. . . the spades on cards aren't for digging

Cards have been used for fortune telling for centuries, especially tarot decks with cards bearing names such as Death, Good Fortune, etc. Hence the expression meaning that something is bound to happen: ON THE CARDS or IN THE CARDS.

There are several astrological links between tarot cards and modern playing cards. The four suits of tarot cards and their meanings have evolved over time. These have included overt male and female sexual symbolism, royalty and magic. By the Middle Ages they represented four elements of society: Knights, the Church, Peasants and Merchants.

Knights were a vital part of medieval society, and were initially represented in tarot cards by swords – which in turn, as phallic symbols, represented males – and named after the Italian word for sword, *spada*. In France, knights were increasingly associated with spears and lances, and so the sword blade became the shape of the point of a long spear or pike. In England this shape, together with a misunderstanding of the word *spada*, led to the symbol becoming more like a shovel/spade shape. Hence we called the suit SPADES. In Italy and in tarot cards across Europe the symbol of the suit is still traditionally a sword.

Another suit was originally represented by cups or chalices, representing the curvy female figure in shape and, as a receptacle, complementing the male spade. Over time this suit evolved into a more overtly feminine image representing love in its widest sense, including the church and the love of God. We know it as HEARTS.

Originally representing the royal sceptre, the symbol of the third suit shifted from a royal mace of authority to a military mace and then to a cudgel. In Italy it is called *batas*, meaning a club. The Latin word *batas* is closely related to our words 'bat', 'beat' and 'batter'. By the time the suit reached France, it had reverted back towards a royal mace topped with a trefoil or *fleur de lis* – the symbol of the French kings. By the time it reached England, the trefoil had been interpreted as a clover leaf and hence this suit came to represent the farmers who brought in the crops and looked after livestock, often associated with clover. However, we adopted the *meaning* of the Italian name for the suit (*batas*) giving us the term CLUBS.

Originally representing coins, the fourth symbol evolved into a pentacle (a five-sided star within a circle) signifying gods, magic and the wealth that they could bestow. The symbol evolved again to a more overtly wealth-related symbol that also came to represent the merchant class within society: DIAMONDS.

The classic pictures of kings on playing cards are stylized representations of four real kings, all of them considered role models in one sense or another. The first king is depicted with the giant sword of Goliath, whom he slew when a shepherd boy, and a harp which he is famous for playing: he is DAVID, KING OF ISRAEL. The second is depicted with clothes adorned with stars, because he wore such clothes during his ten-year campaign across the Middle East: he is ALEXANDER THE GREAT. The third 'king' is always shown in profile, as he was on coins that were distributed throughout the empire he created, although technically he was never a king or an emperor. He is JULIUS CAESAR. The fourth is the King of the Franks and Holy Roman Emperor, always depicted carrying the handle of the sword as protector of the heart of Christ and the Holy Roman Empire: he is King Charles the Great: in Latin, Carolus Magnus, better known to us as CHARLEMAGNE. Incidentally, the queen cards have represented different historical queens and characters from the Bible, but the detail varies from country to country and through the ages.

The English word for cards with the value of two has evolved from Old French *dues* as DEUCE. Similarly, cards with the value of three are called TREYS from *tres*.

Well, I never knew that . . .
. . . if you play against a sharp it probably won't be
worth the candle

Before the days of gas or electric light, some people playing cards would employ boys to hold candles behind them so they could see their cards properly. This is because candles on the table would cast shadows and would often make it more difficult to read the cards they held. At the end of the evening they would need to pay the boy and for the price of the candle itself. If they had not won money that evening, it would have NOT BEEN WORTH THE CANDLE or NOT WORTH A LIGHT.

During the 16th century the word 'envy' began to be used in the sense of challenging another gambler to accept a bet, in the sense that if they won, others would be envious of them. Over time the word was shortened and came to be used to refer to any challenge between two parties: VIE.

Also in the 16th century, in an attempt both to reduce gambling and to raise money for the Treasury, a tax of two shillings and sixpence was applied to every pack of playing cards. This was equivalent to what many people would earn in a week. Because the tax was so high, it was paid only when the cards were actually sold, when the 'tax paid' sign would be stamped on one of the cards. This was done by making one ace symbol much bigger than normal and leaving the centre unprinted so the stamp could be applied. The card traditionally used was THE ACE OF SPADES. When the tax was stopped the printers did not want to change the style and so made use of the space by printing their own details in it. This is why the printer's details often appear on the ace of spades.

'Sharp' was an old word meaning alert and clever, with the implication of taking advantage of other, slower people. Hence when someone is sailing too close to the wind for most people's morals we say he is engaging in SHARP PRACTICE, and someone who cheats at cards is a CARD SHARP. This has sometimes been misheard or reinterpreted as CARD SHARK.

Well, I never knew that . . .
. . . if you've got a Yarborough you can come up trumps
without any trumps!

In many card games you need to play a card that is the same suit as that of the first card played: FOLLOW SUIT.

One card game, originally called triumph, evolved through several names, including whisk, due to the flamboyant way that some players would pick up with a flourish the cards they had won. Confusion with another word meaning 'hush' led to the name by which we know the game today: WHIST (from 'whisht', meaning 'hush'). Meanwhile, the earlier name gave us one of the phrases used within the game: TO TRUMP (meaning to triumph). Trump cards, that is, cards from the suit selected as 'trumps' for that round, beat any non-trump card and so are highly prized. Hence, by analogy of being dealt such a card, receiving good fortune or achieving a good outcome is called COMING UP TRUMPS.

In the 18th century Edmond Hoyle wrote a book detailing the then rules of whist. It proved very popular, as there had been several variations of the rules up to that time. He then published other books on other games, all of which came to be accepted as the definitive rules. An expression subsequently emerged meaning that something is the correct interpretation of the rules: ACCORDING TO HOYLE.

Lord Yarborough was a very keen bridge player and an active gambler. He used to offer anyone odds of 1,000 to 1 that they would not be dealt a hand with no trumps. From this such a hand is called A YARBOROUGH.

If you suspect someone is trying to look at your cards, you may be tempted to hold them up against your body to prevent him or her seeing them. This has given us a phrase for being guarded and reticent about anything: KEEPING YOUR CARDS CLOSE TO YOUR CHEST.

When all cards have been dealt in whist or bridge each player has 13 cards, which is just about as many as anyone can hold comfortably in one hand. When all cards have been played and they are then dealt out again it is therefore called a new HAND.

'Having a game in their hand' is an expression that referred to a player having been dealt exceptionally good cards, so that he could see that he would easily win the game. This has now evolved into A GAME IN HAND, meaning he can see a further victory ahead of him. From the same source we get an even shorter expression meaning that a situation is under control: IN HAND.

Another phrase for being in control of a situation derives from a player ending up with every one of the key cards in the game: he is then said to be HOLDING ALL THE CARDS.

In bridge, spades is the highest-ranking and highest-scoring suit, and so whatever value of cards you have, spades will be the preferred suit. Hence an expression for being in a strong position or having an ample helping of a quality or advantage: TO HAVE IT IN SPADES.

Several sports have taken a phrase from bridge which is used when one team has won all 13 tricks in a hand and jubilantly bangs the last winning card down on the table. It means winning everything that can be won: a GRAND SLAM.

Well, I never knew that . . .
. . . you've got to chip in if you want to hit the jackpot

From the Latin *caspa*, meaning 'a box', *casa* became the Italian word for a house. Thus the North African port where most of the houses were white was called CASABLANCA. From illegal gambling carried out secretly in a small box-room hidden within a house we get the diminutive of *casa*, CASINO. The French word for a wheel is *roue*. And so one of the casino games which is based around a small, spinning wheel is called ROULETTE.

Roulette tables have four very popular betting areas, each of which pays back the original stake plus the same amount again. Two are the colours red and black, usually labelled in French, *rouge* and *noir*. The other two use the Latin-derived terms for even: PAIR (from *par*, meaning equal) and the term for odd, the opposite of pair: IMPAIR.

In early card games, coins that were being bet were literally put into a central bowl, and the winner would then take all its contents. Hence the term THE POT.

In an early variant of poker a special 'pot' of money was gradually increased through the game until a player had a pair of *jacks*. He could then claim this money even if he did not win the hand. Hence the phrase has become associated with winning a lot of 'bonus' money not associated with skill: HIT THE JACKPOT.

The idea of having to put a couple of coins into the pot before being able to participate also gives us the phrase used in discussion when seeking permission to contribute or participate: 'CAN I PUT MY TWO PENNYWORTH IN?' or, in the States, 'CAN I PUT MY TWO BITS/CENTS IN?'

Incidentally, the US term 'two bits', meaning 25 cents, has an interesting derivation. Back in medieval England, coins were made of precious metals and were actually worth their face value. Therefore a shilling coin could be cut into quarters and each quarter would be worth three pennies. As they were pieces of a larger coin, they were called threepenny BITS (of a shilling). The UK retained this term for coins with straight edges right up to the 1960s. The US dollar coin was actually based upon a Spanish coin that was worth eight *real* (a Spanish unit of currency). These coins are best known by the pirate term PIECES OF EIGHT. In theory one of these coins could be cut into eight pieces, each worth one *real* or 12.5 cents. However, 25 cents was much easier to work with; hence the term TWO BITS, meaning a quarter of a dollar.

In the game of blackjack a player can, in theory at least, get the odds in his favour by counting how many picture cards have been played and how many low-value cards have been played. The significance of this is that if there are more picture cards than low-value cards still to play, there is more chance of the dealer losing each hand. This technique, which is banned in most casinos, is called COUNTING, and a gambler suspected of using this trick will often be asked to leave.

Professional gamblers have come up with all sorts of theories to beat casinos. Some have succeeded, whether by spotting a fault with a roulette wheel that means that some numbers come up more frequently than they should, or 'counting' the cards at blackjack, or using hidden electronic devices to enable covert teams to get the odds into their favour. The idea of trying to make money from casinos has led to a phrase that nowadays is used to describe people who make money through acting as some form of middle-man or big business deal-maker. Originally, though, it referred to the two most popular activities in casinos, roulette and cards: WHEELER DEALERS.

Two phrases meaning it is time to give up come from gambling. You do not gamble with cash in casinos; you buy chips at the start of the evening and then, at the end of the evening, you convert whatever chips you have back into cash: CASH IN YOUR CHIPS. If you have spent your money and used up all your tokens you have HAD YOUR CHIPS.

In poker and other betting games it is usually necessary in casinos for players to put chips into a central pot in order to play; thus contributing to a central pot or resource of any kind is called CHIPPING IN.

When a casino gambler places a bet he puts his betting tokens (chips) onto the table. For example, in roulette he places them on the number he believes will win. Having placed his chips he is not allowed to move them again. From this we get the phrase meaning that an irreversible commitment has been made regarding a risky situation and that there is great anticipation to see the outcome: THE CHIPS ARE DOWN.

In a casino, if you bet everything you will often push a whole pile of chips into play, leaving no reserve. You do so by pushing the bottom of the pile and hence are BETTING YOUR BOTTOM DOLLAR.

During the great depression of the late 1920s and early 1930s there were few people who were in a position to use the highest-denomination betting tokens, which were usually coloured blue. Those people who could were clearly extremely wealthy and secure in their financial situation, despite the worry and uncertainty in the economy. A small number of large companies were also seen as very well run, with solid financial backing and good prospects for the future. These companies became known as BLUE-CHIP COMPANIES.

Well, I never knew that . . .
. . . you can bet money or meat – it's the same word

The ancient word *steg* meaning 'to pierce' led to our word for a piece of wood that could be used to pierce something: a STICK. It also gave us the word for a piece of meat that could be cooked by being pierced with a stick and held over a fire: STEAK. A large 'stick' could also be STUCK in the ground and used as a pole, giving us the word STAKE. Short stakes would often be set up at temporary markets where people would finalize details of trading deals or bets. The cash involved would be placed in a dish on top of these pieces of wood. Hence the term for money being bet: STAKE. In permanent markets these stakes would be made of metal, and because of their resemblance in shape to giant nails they were called NAILS. Deals done here would require cash payment immediately. Hence the phrase PAY ON THE NAIL.

Incidentally, because small, sharpened sticks were used to 'pin' two documents together, we get the verb TO STICK things together. When adhesives became available to glue things together, we kept the same word, even though sticks are no longer involved!

At the end of betting in the game of poker, despite whatever bluffing has been going on, in order to beat someone else's cards you need to declare what cards you actually have. This gives us a phrase now used more widely to mean showing your true resources or intentions: SHOWING YOUR HAND. Alternatively, if you believe that you will inevitably be beaten, instead of showing your hand you give up and THROW IN YOUR HAND.

If you want to keep the betting going during a game of poker it is necessary to raise the stake by at least one more coin. Hence the phrase TO GO ONE BETTER.

The Latin word meaning 'in front' is used in poker and other games where a player needs to provide money up front in order to play or stay in the game. The word is ANTE. If a player is very confident or wishes to intimidate someone else out of the game he can increase the amount of money necessary to stay in the game: UP THE ANTE. Incidentally, the same word is used in Italian restaurants to describe the course that precedes the main pasta course: ANTIPASTA.

Medieval fairground games would sometimes have a hen as a prize. From the French name for a hen (*poule*) we get the word for a prize in betting games, especially card games: the POOL. When such a pool is won, the winner will sometimes sweep his winnings to his side of the table in a dramatic way, giving rise to the phrase nowadays  used more widely to mean having won everything: SWEEPING THE BOARD. A related phrase is used to describe betting among a group of friends who agree that one of them will end up with the entire pot of all the stakes bid: SWEEPSTAKE.

In early US gambling houses there was usually a slot or 'hole' in the table, into which the dealer would slip money which then fell through into a locked drawer. To get the first card dealt each player would have to pay a certain amount. This first card was played face down, because you had paid money to be in the game. It was called THE HOLE CARD, an expression in America nowadays meaning something secret. Clearly, the higher this card is the better, hence the expression meaning having something important in reserve: having an ACE IN THE HOLE. Equally, if a gambler was allowed credit by the gambling house he would be said to be IN THE HOLE – meaning owing someone money, probably more than he could really afford.

When playing cards one should always keep one's cards in clear view of everyone else. If one's hands go out of sight under the table it is considered UNDERHAND. Rather, they should be kept above the table or ABOVE BOARD.

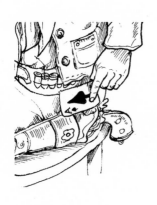

In poker, the dealer would often have a knife on the table in front of him to make it clear who was dealing. In the Wild West these knives would often have handles made from the horn of a buck (deer). When it was time to pass on the responsibility of being the dealer to the next player, the retiring dealer would literally PASS THE BUCK. When American President Harry S. Truman wanted to demonstrate his leadership and responsibility he famously said 'THE BUCK STOPS HERE'. Sometimes a silver dollar would be used as a marker, and through this association we get the slang term for a dollar: A BUCK.

At the end of the 19th century a carpenter in Lancashire developed a local game also called 'buck' into a very popular pub game. It came to real prominence in 1908 when a pub landlord was accused of letting people play a game of chance in his pub – which was not allowed. By soundly beating a court official at the game in the courtroom he proved that it was in fact a game of skill! Ever since it has remained a very popular pub game, and has hardly changed – except for its name. We call it DARTS.

During the 15th and 16th centuries people would bet on almost anything, so if a situation arose in a game where it was considered that both parties had a roughly equal chance of winning, bets would be offered between the players and observers where the odds were 'divided equally' – in Latin, *iu parti*. This phrase began to be used in Britain to describe an uncertain outcome and, increasingly through the 17th century, a situation of risk and then potential danger. In parallel the letter 'i' evolved into two forms, one remaining 'i' the other lengthening its stalk and becoming a new letter: 'j'. This is exactly what happened to the 'i' at the front of *iu parti*, which became *ju parti* and eventually evolved into our word JEOPARDY.

Well, I never knew that . . .
. . . if you get left in the lurch it will be a long time
before you peg out

The card game of cribbage used to be very popular in Britain in the 19th century. In this game you record your scores by moving small wooden or ivory pegs around the board. You win by getting your counting peg all the way off the board and out of the playing area. You then stop playing. This has given us the phrase meaning to be finished or to die: TO PEG OUT.

In cribbage, 'lurch' is the word used to describe the situation when one player is so far behind that it is most unlikely that he can win – for example, if one player has scored 51 points and the other player has not even reached the first corner of the board. This gives us the expression TO BE LEFT IN THE LURCH, meaning being in a very disadvantageous position from which one is unlikely to recover. When two players have the same score this will be obvious by the positioning of their counting pegs; hence LEVEL PEGGING.

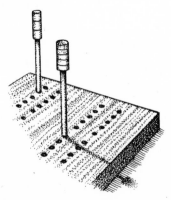

When playing dice it does not take long to have one or even two goes. Hence the expression 'I WILL BE FINISHED IN A COUPLE OF SHAKES'.

During the long and boring siege of a Saracen fortress called Hasart, 12th-century crusaders adopted a local dice game. The Arabic word for chance was *alzahr*, and the two words were combined to name the dice game. The crusaders brought the game back to the UK, where it became very popular until eventually the government banned it from London because whole fortunes were being bet, won and lost through it. The name of the game evolved into a word that then became strongly associated with high-risk outcomes: HAZARD (from Hasart and *alzahr*).

A form of raffle is named after the *tumbling* motion of slips of paper in a rotating box that ensures a random selection: TOMBOLA.

Scores in many games, especially in pubs, would often be recorded by chalking them on the ground or wall. The higher the score, the more chalk marks. If you won with a lot more chalk marks you would be said to WIN BY A LONG CHALK.

In the early 19th century a book was written that told how an Irishman bet that he could create a new word and get it used by the whole population of Dublin within 24 hours. That night he had four letters written up all over the city. It was very similar to the Latin words *qui es*, meaning 'Who is it?' The next day everyone was saying the word to see if anyone knew what it meant – so he won the bet! The word has subsequently been used for asking questions, initially about what something means, but nowadays on a wider basis, as in pub competitions and on television shows. The letters were Q-U-I-Z, and the new word was QUIZ. This is also the origin of this series of books. See page 239 for more information! **WINKT!**

10

Kids' Games, Pub Games and Board Games

We've all played games as children, and to a lesser extent go on doing so throughout our lives; so it is not surprising that we find many more phrases have entered our language from such activities.

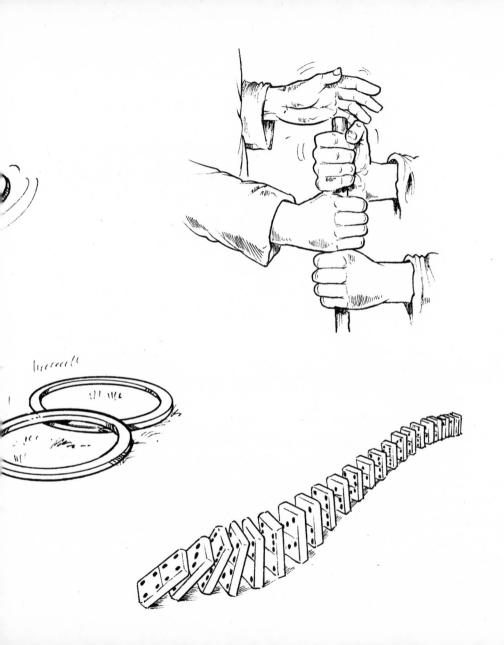

Well, I never knew that . . .
. . . being game is no fun if you're a deer

Man is a very old Indo-European word meaning just that, a man. Combined with another ancient word, *ga,* meaning 'together', it gave the medieval word *gammen* that means men doing things together or participating, from which we get the word GAME. By the 13th century this word was associated with leisure-time activities and with someone's willingness to join in. Hence the phrase 'ARE YOU GAME ENOUGH (to join in)?' This idea of pluckiness was then applied to animals when they were hunted, in the sense of giving the hunters a good and satisfying challenge. From here the word was applied to a variety of animals that the nobility would hunt in the private parks, such as deer, pheasant, etc., giving us the new meaning of the word GAME.

There is an Arabic game consisting of four different parts to the board, each called a 'table'. Hence the game was initially called TABLES. In this game pieces can suddenly be moved back to a less advantageous table and so the outcome of the game can suddenly change when THE TABLES ARE TURNED. This feature, that pieces can in fact be forced to go *backwards*, gave the game its current name: BACKGAMMON, from *back gammen*, meaning the game that can go backwards. Backgammon is a betting game where each player can double the stakes when he feels confident he will win. Occasionally, though, a lucky dice throw can enable a player who was losing suddenly to take a winning position. Such a reversal clearly gives the ultimate winner the benefit of the loser's earlier misplaced confidence. Of course, if a player does not wish to accept the doubled stakes he has the option of surrendering the game: DOUBLE OR QUITS.

An old Oxfordshire game, still played in some of the county's pubs, involves contestants throwing a heavy stick at a representation of an old lady's head. This can be anything from a simple log to a model with a discernible nose and occasionally a pipe. More usually it is now another stick with a rounded top, called a doll. From the habit of one person putting the target in position and then others seeing if they can knock it down, the name of the game has now come to be used in discussions where someone proposes an outline idea which others question to see if the idea can 'stand up' to criticism. The game and the phrase are both called AUNT SALLY.

The old children's fairground game of having to throw a wooden hoop over a stick that stuck up out of the ground (that is, was cocked) to win a prize gives us the phrase for being very happy: COCK A HOOP.

The Old Saxon word *fyllan*, meaning 'to strike down', has given us the word for chopping down a tree: TO FELL. This word was also used to describe the punishment of blinding a convicted criminal, as he was 'struck down' with blindness by having his eyes gouged out. This has given us a term used in games where one or more players are prevented from seeing by strips of cloth being tied round their faces to simulate being 'struck down' with blindness, giving us the word BLINDFOLD (from *blindfellen*).

In medieval days there was a forerunner of a modern party game in which one player was blindfolded and then had to chase after a specific player who was also blindfolded while fending off *buffeting* from other players. The rules have evolved but the name is still the same: BLIND MAN'S BUFF. Incidentally, the word 'buffeting' comes from the French *buffe*, meaning blow.

In the Middle Ages children had no coins and so when trying to choose someone randomly they could not toss a coin. Instead they would often pick up a stick and grasp it at the bottom. Another child grabbed it just above their hand, and so on until the last hand grabbed the very top bit. This person, who won the privilege of starting first, was described as having THE UPPER HAND.

A game originated in China over 2000 years ago and came to Britain as trade increased during the early 18th century. Its original name in the UK, 'Janken', referred back to its Chinese heritage, although nowadays it is better known by the elements of the game in which each of three options can be beaten by one other and can beat the third: CHIN–CHAN–CHINAMAN or SCISSORS, PAPER, STONE.

Children have always loved playing with words to create fun rhymes. This has given us several 'nonsense' phrases, although each has its own logical origin. For example, the old phrase *wile he* (from *willan*, 'to will') meant: Does he will/wish to do something? This was combined with *ne* (from French meaning 'not') to give the opposite – 'ne wile he', meaning he does not will/wish to do something. Hence we get the phrase meaning that something will happen whether or not a person wants it to happen: WILLY NILLY. In a similar way you can imagine an uncertain child saying, 'Shall I? Shall I? Shall I?' becoming the more musical 'Shall I? Shill I? Shall I? Shill I?' – or, as we know it, SHILLY-SHALLYING. Equally, we have a phrase for the idea of a child pointlessly dallying around and then being told off for DILLY-DALLYING.

Well, I never knew that . . .

. . . you can't knuckle down if you've lost your marbles

The game of marbles used to be very popular and would often include betting on who would win. In these circumstances it was important that the players adhered strictly to the rules, especially the rule that the player's knuckle must be placed in the correct position on the ground. Players who did not concentrate upon following this rule would be chastised with a phrase we use to get people to concentrate upon the task in hand: 'KNUCKLE DOWN!'

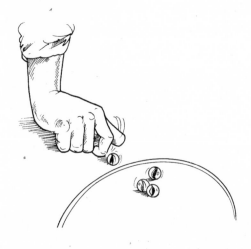

Collecting marbles used to be very popular with young boys, with different colours, patterns and sizes being very sought after. So if a boy misplaced his favourite marbles – or, even worse, if they were stolen – he would get extremely upset and irrational, having LOST HIS MARBLES.

In the 1930s two Danes started selling wooden toys under a brand name that meant 'play well' in Danish. The toys proved popular, and when they started using a new plastic material during the late 1950s sales really took off. In particular, their interchangeable building blocks were extremely popular and by the 1960s this toy was successful internationally. By the year 2000 well over 100 billion bricks had been made. The original Danish phrase was *leg godt*, and the game was branded as LEGO. Incidentally, the founders of the company were against war, which is why there are very few bricks of two colours even to this day. The reason is that, without bricks coloured GREEN AND BROWN, children cannot make realistic camouflaged tanks and 'play' at war.

In the 1980s a game was developed involving a computerized puck moving around a maze. The game had originally been intended to be called Puckman. However, there was concern that the letter 'P' could be altered to leave a very embarrassing word and so the name was adapted and the puck was converted into a little monster named PACMAN.

A craze of the late 1990s was based upon collecting toys and trading cards of *monsters* that could be kept in your *pocket*: POKEMON or 'pocket monster'. Each monster's name had some unusual but traceable derivation. Hence two martial arts creatures were called Hit Man Lee, based upon CHRISTOPHER LEE, and Hit Man Chan, based on JACKIE CHAN. The snake monsters were called ARBOK (from 'cobra' backwards) and EKANS ('snake' backwards). The craze spawned computer games, card collecting, a TV series, three feature-length cartoon films and massive merchandizing.

When dominos are set up on end, if one falls over it knocks over all the others in a chain reaction; hence we have what is called THE DOMINO EFFECT. Incidentally, in 2004 a new world

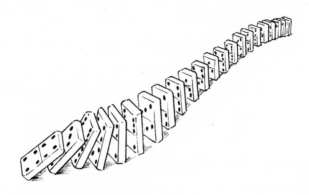

record was achieved for the most dominoes set up and successfully toppled. It took a team of 81 people to do it and they toppled 3,992,397 dominoes in one go! Now, that is a lot of domino effect!

Well, I never knew that . . .
. . . in the jungle or the city, you can still be sent back to
square one

While séances of one form or another have been around since the Stone Age, it was only in Victorian times that a séance board was formally manufactured and patented. It was designed to allow questions to be answered with a 'yes' or a 'no'. Its name derived from the answer to the question 'Is anybody there?' using the French and German words for 'yes': OUIJA (*Oui* in French and *Ja* in German), though it was often referred to as 'OUIJI'.

When playing a board game, you sometimes end up just one square away from winning, needing a score of just one next time round to get you 'home'. A one on a dice used to be called the 'ace', hence the phrase WITHIN AN ACE OF SOMETHING.

Two thousand years ago in India a game was designed to educate children about good and evil. The winner was the person who first reached the Nirvana square at the top of the board. To get there players tried to land on good squares such as 'generosity', 'knowledge' or 'faith'. When they did so they advanced along short cuts towards Nirvana. When they landed on evil squares such as 'theft', 'vanity', 'lust' or 'greed', they were attacked by jungle animals and had to move backwards away from Nirvana. To teach children about the many dangers in the world there were more evil squares than good ones. However, when the game came to Britain in the 19th century the names of the squares were changed to Victorian virtues and vices. For example, landing on the square marked 'industrious' led to advancement to a square called 'success'; landing on 'indulgence' led down to 'poverty'. The number of good and bad squares were also equalized to improve the run of play. Since then the names have disappeared, although other elements of the game, such as the Indian jungle animals, are clearly recognizable to this day in SNAKES AND LADDERS. This game also gave rise to another saying meaning having to return to the start, as in some versions of the game this is exactly what happened when you landed on a square called disobedience: BACK TO SQUARE ONE.

In the middle of the great depression of the 1930s a heating engineer called Charles Darrow designed a game based on the streets of Atlantic City, New Jersey, where he regularly took his family on holiday. It reflected the frequent change of ownership of buildings as landlords fell upon hard times and other landlords then developed new buildings. The game was not an immediate success but has since become very well known, especially for different versions made for different cities around the world. It is MONOPOLY.

In Monopoly, statistically the most frequently landed upon set is the ORANGE SET. In the London game this consists of Vine Street, Marlborough Street and Bow Street. This is because when people come out of jail, more than one in three dice throws will move a piece to one of these squares. In fact, the most frequently landed-on square through dice throws is the COMMUNITY CHEST (between Marlborough Street and Bow Street). This is because the most common score from throwing two dice is seven, and it is seven squares from jail. The most common square to end your turn upon in Monopoly is JAIL – by landing on the square itself, by being sent there by a card you pick up, by throwing three successive doubles, or by landing on the GO TO JAIL square.

Another well-known board game is named after the Latin word for 'I play': LUDO. **WINKT!**

APPENDIX I

Bonus extract taken from
DID COWBOYS INVENT BRANDING?
Well, I Never Knew That!
BIG BUSINESS AND GREAT BRANDS

ISBN 978-0-9551525-4-2

Chess, Checkmate and the Exchequer!

Who would have thought that a Chinese game has given us checklists, a government minister, a method of payment, an excuse to not date someone, pubs and even patterned cloth?

Well it has – read on!

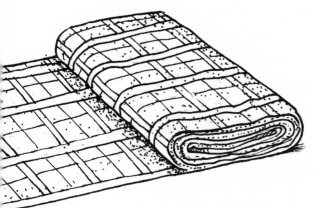

Luigi's

Starters $10·00
Main $25·00
Desert $6·00
$41·00
Have a nice day!

THE CHEQUERS

Well, I never knew that . . .
. . . a rook is no bird and the king never dies

T he game of chess, invented in China, was very popular in the Middle East before it came to England. Middle Eastern leaders were named *shah*, in honour of the great Roman leader Caesar. In Arabic, the words *shah mát* (with emphasis upon the second 'a' sound) means 'the king is dead', whereas *shah mat* (with no accent on the second 'a') means the king is *perplexed*. Over time the word *shah* as used in chess evolved in France into *eschec* (meaning 'check'), giving 'eschec mat' and then in England to CHECKMATE. Interestingly, in the version of chess played in the West the

king is never in fact taken – the game finishes where it is threatened and has nowhere to go. That is, he is *perplexed* as opposed to dead! This is because, in the Middle East, from where the game came to us, military coups were commonplace and it was found to be much more pragmatic to capture a king and use him as a puppet ruler than to kill him and risk alienating the whole population. If you are planning an attack but are then put into check you must temporarily put your own plans on hold and respond to the other player's attack. Hence the phrase to have your plans or intentions CHECKED.

The word 'check', from 'checkmate', soon became used to mean an intervention, and from here the specific intervention of approving an action or payment – to 'check' the payment. Subsequently, the mark made in documents to show approval, such as a tick, also took the same word and became a CHECK MARK or simply a CHECK. This is still used by pilots, for example in going through a preflight test of their equipment. Increasingly, documents such as invoices and receipts were also referred to as 'checks', and in America and some other places, when diners at a restaurant want the bill they still ask

for the CHECK. Similarly, if a baseball game was called off due to very bad weather, all the ticket holders would be issued with documents that allowed them to return to see the match when it was rescheduled. The names of these 'receipts' for future games has given rise to a more widely used phrase, often as a polite way of saying no: TAKING A RAIN CHECK.

Back in medieval England, a custom had developed of using a large cloth up to 8 feet square, marked out as a large chessboard, for assessing the finances of the King and the nation and for calculating taxes. This cloth also took its name from the French *eschec* and the English 'check', to give us the word EXCHEQUER. The sheet was used in a similar way to an abacus and gave its name to the part of the government that looked after the nation's finances: the (department of the) Exchequer. The person who handled these finances on behalf of the King was called the CHANCELLOR OF THE EXCHEQUER and still fulfils a vital role in the British government.

The cloth was used as a kind of abacus at every level of tax collection and so they became common throughout the country. Where inns were used as local tax collection points they would sometimes adopt the name to let everyone know of their role and sometimes to offer moneylending services. These inns were often called the Exchequer Cloth, the Exchequer Inn or, later, the Checker Inn or simply the CHEQUERS. Various games other than chess developed using these cloths, the best known adopting the name 'chequers' – also known as draughts. Eventually the cloths were replaced with wooden boards, giving us the term CHEQUER BOARD. When material was made for clothes with a similar pattern involving parallel sets of lines crossing each other it was also

called CHEQUERED, although now often we spell it CHECKERED. Given that a chequerboard has a mixture of white and black squares, anyone who has a mixed past with some good (white) and some bad (black) elements is said to have a CHEQUERED PAST. The King would often decide to discuss financial matters of state with his Chancellor away from the hubbub of government, so it is not surprising that the Prime Minister's official residence in the countryside is called CHEQUERS.

When the government committed itself to making payments, the documents themselves were initially called 'exchequer's documents', which over many years was shortened to simply CHEQUES. To help keep a record of these cheques, copies of the documents were made and kept safe in books. At the time the Latin word for leaf (*folio*) was used to describe pages. For example, the idea of turning over a new page in a book to start with a 'clean sheet' was also described as TURNING OVER A NEW LEAF – meaning to start afresh. The idea of the copy being a 'leaf' in a book gives us the word for the name of the stub in a CHEQUE BOOK used to record the details of a used cheque: COUNTERFOIL. While the spelling 'check' remained to describe the action of checking, in the UK the new 'cheque' was adopted for the documents. In the US the old spelling was retained and so they still use 'checks'.

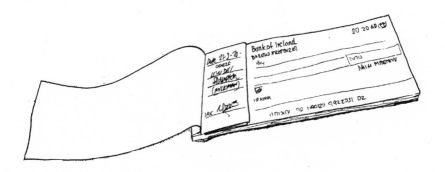

Rukh in Persian means soldier. It is from this word that we get the name for the piece also called a castle: ROOK.

Interestingly, in Chinese chess there is a river cutting the board in half and two castles drawn on the board which the mandarins (kings) cannot leave. The pieces reflect the animals, vehicles and troops in ancient Chinese armies; hence we get elephants, chariots, cavalry, infantry, the mandarins' personal guards and even canons.

In Japanese chess each piece is flat and is marked differently on both sides, giving it different capabilities. When a piece is taken it can in fact be replayed on the board by the opponent the other way up! **WINKT!**

Bonus extract taken from
DID NOAH INVENT TENNIS?
Well, I Never Knew That!
AN HISTORIC MISCELLANY

From Real Tennis to Lawn Tennis

Did you know that we owe the pleasures of
Wimbledon to medieval Moors and monks?
Read on . . .

Well, I never knew that . . .
. . . tennis is scored 'love all, 15, 30, 40, game' because of eggs,
clocks and Noah's Ark!

The medieval Arabs used to play a game in which they hit a ball to each other with their hands. It was initially spread to Spain by the invading Moors and then taken up by Christian knights and churchmen during the crusades of the 11th and 12th centuries. They in turn took it back with them to their homelands, where it became especially popular in the French monasteries. Before one player served, he would shout 'Take this!' – or, in French, 'Tenez!' Over time the word, and the activity, evolved into an early form of what in England we call TENNIS.

In the monasteries the game was played in the courtyards, hence the phrase TENNIS COURT.

Henry VIII played a great deal of this game at his purpose-built tennis courtyard in HAMPTON COURT.

The Latin word *regalis* (meaning royal) evolved into a shorter word both in Spain, where it is still used today, and in England, where it is used only in conjunction with this form of tennis, giving us REAL TENNIS. Incidentally, in Spain the word is used, for example, to describe the 'royal' city of Madrid where the King lived: REAL MADRID.

The monastic courtyards would usually have sloping roofs over the surrounding passageways or cloisters, held up by pillars. This is still used as the basic design of real tennis courts. Initially a piece of rope was strung across the courtyard to divide it into two parts, with each player needing to play into his opponent's area. Hence the phrase THE BALL IS IN YOUR COURT – nowadays meaning 'it is now your turn or responsibility'.

To make it easier to see who won the point, the rope evolved into a net. Where necessary, posts would be sunk into the ground from which the net was hung. One strategy in the game can be to play close to the net with one shot and then to the back of the court near the pillars of the old cloisters, and so on, to wear your opponent out. Hence the phrase FROM PILLAR TO POST, meaning running all over the place.

In real tennis it is important to make the ball bounce as close to certain lines as possible. This creates an advantage called a 'chase' that can, in fact, suddenly win a game. This can best be achieved by hitting the ball with the racquet at a sharp (cutting) angle, a tactic which gives us the phrase to CUT TO THE CHASE – to come to the point immediately.

Monks would make balls out of cloth tied with string and initially used their hands to hit the ball. Hence the different terms for hitting a ball: BACKHAND and FOREHAND. In France a version of the game is still called *jeu de paume* – the game of the palm.

To avoid hurting their hands, players often copied the Arabic tradition of wrapping a length of cloth called *ruqatwas* around their hand. This gives us the word RACQUET. Incidentally, the racquet used in real tennis is unique in that it is non-symmetrical and still made from wood rather than carbon fibre. It is shaped like a giant palm with one side flat, representing the part next to the little finger, and one side rounded, like the side where the thumb is.

Scoring was done using the quarter-hours on the monastery clock, which is how we have ended up with 15, 30, 45 AND GAME. The third number, however, was close to another

number that had strong biblical connections and so it was changed to that number: 40. It rained on the ark for 40 days and 40 nights; Moses went to Mount Sinai for 40 days; Jesus was in the wilderness for 40 days; and so on. The shape of an egg gives rise to the word describing a nil score: LOVE, from *l'oeuf*, French for egg, and the shape of zero. The shape of an egg has also given rise to different phrases for a score of zero in ball games: in the UK a DUCK, in the US a GOOSE. Also, when someone tries something that does not work it can be said that they have just LAID AN EGG, meaning they have produced zero benefit.

When two tennis players tied at a score of 40, it was agreed that instead of just one more point to win, either player would need two clear points to win. Thus we get the word DEUCE – from *deux*, French for two.

Given the nature of the original cloisters, with gaps between the pillars, a rule developed that is still key to real tennis that the ball must always be served so that it makes contact with a roof first and then drops down into the court. Because different monasteries had different shaped courtyards there was no standard court. However, the game always involved hitting balls onto various roofs and walls, and part of the skill was trying to anticipate the unpredictable angles at which the ball would rebound off them. This gives us the phrase OFF THE WALL, meaning an unusual angle, or new idea.

In tennis, and some other sports, players can be ranked by their likelihood of winning, so that matches can be arranged to avoid leading players meeting one another in the early rounds of a competition, so saving the closest-fought matches for the later rounds. Using an analogy with the gardener's practice of carefully spacing plants to avoid unnecessary competition for good soil, or premature weeding out of potentially good plants, we get the phrase SEEDING of competitors.

A variety of tennis played in France, called *bande*, ended up having more emphasis upon hitting the ball with the wooden part of the racquet. A similar game in Ireland, with some similarities to lacrosse, involved hitting a wooden object around between players on a flat piece of ground, sometimes played on ice. This game was also called *bande*. From this idea of hitting the ball around among several players we get the phrase BANDIED ABOUT. The stick used was a distinctive shape, having a long straight handle with a flat end bent at a sharp angle. This gave us the phrase for people with bent or bow legs: BANDY-LEGGED. And this game eventually evolved into what we know as hockey.

Incidentally for centuries tennis courts resembling monastic courtyards were built across England. However the sheer cost of doing so eventually led to a new version of the game that could be played in the open without major construction costs. This is what we know as LAWN TENNIS!   **WINKT!**

Bonus extract taken from
DID NOAH INVENT TENNIS?
Well, I Never Knew That!
AN HISTORIC MISCELLANY

From Brawling to Boxing

Life has a way of handing out some
hard knocks, so perhaps it's not
surprising that fighting sports have
given us a lot of phrases we use
without ever going near a boxing ring!

Well, I never knew that . . .
. . . if you get shirty you might not be laughing when the
punchline comes

In the 19th century, when gentlemen disagreed about something and wished to fight, it was considered unseemly to fight while dressed – that would be too much like common men brawling. So they would at least undress to their shirts, and often remove these as well. Hence the phrase meaning that someone is getting ready for a fight: GETTING SHIRTY. If, however, you preferred to calm things down and avoid a physical confrontation you would say: 'KEEP YOUR SHIRT ON.'

In both boxing and horse racing, contestants have to be weighed before an event and the weight, which is then publicly announced, can significantly affect how people bet on them. It is also a point of no return, after which contestants are wholly committed to going through with the event to the final outcome. From this we get the phrase meaning that someone is committing themselves wholeheartedly to a situation: WEIGHING IN.

In boxing, consistent blows to the body can wear an opponent down, and if the hitter is lucky, such a punch may catch his opponent unguarded and wind him, significantly reducing his ability to fight back. Hence we call any serious impact a BODY BLOW.

To move around the ring boldly poking your chin out as if you are happy for it to be hit and challenging the opponent to try is an act of extreme confidence: TO LEAD WITH THE CHIN. Sometimes a tough boxer does take a hit but doesn't go down. He carries on fighting as if untroubled by the blow, even though it must have hurt him. Hence the phrase we use for someone who suffers criticism, a setback or a firm rebuke, but accepts it and carries on anyway: TAKING IT ON THE CHIN.

When a person is convulsed with laughter, after hearing the end of a good joke, he often grabs his belly, as if he had been hit in the gut: so we call the climax of the joke the PUNCHLINE.

Well, I never knew that . . .
. . . losing your bottle means you won't
come up to scratch

In the days of bare-knuckle boxing there were very few rules. One of them was that two lines would be scratched in the mud a few feet apart, and then each boxer would put the tip of one foot up against the line before commencing the

fight, so that he was TOEING THE LINE. If one boxer was knocked down or if the referee had to restart the fight, both boxers had to put their foot on the line again within 30 seconds or lose the match; if one of them didn't, then he hadn't COME UP TO [THE] SCRATCH. Also, from the referee's instruction for boxers to get ready, 'get set to the scratch', we have a phrase that simply means a fight:

a SET TO. Later, a time limit of ten seconds was set for a boxer to get back on his feet or lose the fight; if he didn't get up then, he was OUT FOR THE COUNT. If a boxer is knocked down, possibly rendered unconscious, and counted out before he can regain his feet, he has clearly lost the fight and is DOWN AND OUT. Another meaning of the same phrase is that someone has fallen upon very hard times and is probably living below their previous station in life: 'down in life and out of luck'.

When we want to say that something fits the bill completely, we use the phrase created to describe a fighter who comes to the mark in the ground confidently, when told to do so by the referee, looking fit and ready for the fight: he was said to have

COME UP TO THE MARK. Likewise, when we think that someone's behaviour is beyond the limits of acceptability, we describe it in the same way as a boxer who is so keen to start the fight that he steps forward past the mark in the ground before the referee has signalled the start of the round: he is said to have OVERSTEPPED THE MARK.

A lot of money could be bet on boxing matches, and so if a decision was marginal there would often be a great deal of argument and shouting to try to get the judges to change their minds. Of course, this did not happen as everyone knew that the decisions were final and not open to discussion. Nevertheless, the arguments would carry on, giving us the expression ALL OVER BAR THE SHOUTING.

Boxing is a very strenuous activity, leading to dehydration, so boxers need a lot of water, and the bottle of water was an important part of a boxer's support. If a boxer was getting injured and losing a fight, his seconds would sometime use a phrase meaning that he could not carry on: he had LOST HIS BOTTLE. We use the same phrase today to mean that someone has lost his nerve.

If a boxer was clearly taking a beating and the bell sounded to end the round, allowing him a short time in which to recover, it was said that he had been SAVED BY THE BELL. However, once it became clear that he was going to lose the fight, his seconds could accept defeat by tossing a towel into the centre of the ring – THROWING IN THE TOWEL. And

sometimes a boxer who had had enough would say 'COUNT ME OUT' – as we do nowadays when we want to withdraw from something.

At fairgrounds, bare-knuckle boxers would issues challenges to all-comers, with cash prizes for the winner. Those who accepted the challenge would pitch their hats into the fighting arena. From this we get the phrase THROWING YOUR HAT INTO THE RING.

To avoid serious injuries, gloves were gradually introduced and eventually bare-knuckle boxing was outlawed. However, occasionally two fighters who hated each other would

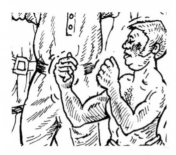

sometimes revert to the more dangerous form of fighting. Hence the phrase THE GLOVES ARE OFF, or TO TAKE ONE'S GLOVES OFF – meaning making a confrontation more aggressive and doing the most to harm the other side.

In boxing, if you are losing, tired and battered, there is a tendency to avoid fighting and to back away around the ring; but, as the saying goes, YOU CAN RUN BUT YOU CAN'T HIDE. Sometimes a tired boxer would fall back onto the ropes around the edge of the ring, from where we get the phrase ON THE ROPES to refer to someone who is really up against it.

Over two thousand years ago Herodotus, one of the greatest commentators of the ancient world, said: 'The thunderbolts of the gods chastise the more enormous animals!' At the start of the 20th century Bob Fitzsimmons, a small boxer who was famous for beating bigger opponents, was asked if he was intimidated by larger boxers. He famously replied: 'THE BIGGER THEY ARE, THE HARDER THEY FALL' – which became his catchphrase.

Well, I never knew that . . .
. . . if you fight by London Rules you don't pull your punches

From the wooden blocks shaped like heads on which wigs used to be displayed we get the term for a head: BLOCK. For example, someone who is as unintelligent as a piece of wood is called a BLOCKHEAD. And someone warning a boxer against sticking his chin out would say: 'IF YOU STICK YOUR NECK OUT YOU WILL GET YOUR BLOCK KNOCKED OFF.' This has given rise to shorter sayings: "DON'T STICK YOUR NECK OUT" and "I'LL KNOCK YOUR BLOCK OFF".

Bare-knuckle fights would always result in bleeding injuries to the face and to the boxers' own hands, as bone crunched into bone. The skin and flesh round the knuckles would often

be particularly badly torn, with the bones almost showing through. Hence the phrase NEAR THE KNUCKLE.

A full power punch is delivered with the boxer's full body-weight behind it. An alternative is to pull back at the last moment to either land a much lighter punch or not make any contact at all: TO PULL ONE'S PUNCHES.

In boxing, blows can come up from below – an UPPER CUT – or be delivered directly with a horizontal blow, like a direct and honest statement: STRAIGHT FROM THE SHOULDER.

When a person has completed what he or she set out to do, despite the difficulties encountered along the way, they are described in the same way as a boxer who sees a fight through to the end of the final round: he is said to have GONE THE DISTANCE.

Boxers are classified into categories of weights to ensure approximately fair and safe contests. One very light weight category in boxing is named after a very aggressive and plucky but small breed of chicken found in south-east Asia: BANTAM weight. If a boxer successfully takes on an opponent from a higher weight category he is said to be PUNCHING ABOVE HIS WEIGHT.

Around 1840 new rules were introduced to focus fights on boxing instead of gouging, kicking or head-butting. However,

the audiences in London preferred to see the blood and dirty tricks, and so the rules were usually ignored there. Hence a term came to mean that no rules would be applied: LONDON RULES.

In 1867 a new set of the standard rules of boxing were drawn up to govern the sport in Britain. They were endorsed and named after John Sholto Douglas, better known by his aristocratic title, the Marquess of Queensberry. Hence the new regulations were called the QUEENSBERRY RULES. Among other things, they prohibited punches aimed anywhere near the groin. Hence the phrase for any action or comment that hurts someone else (physically or not) but is considered cheating: BELOW THE BELT.   **WINKT!**

Thank you for reading this book. I do hope you said ...

Please read on and find out about:

- Locating your favourite phrases from the Index.

- How you can help make a brand new word.

- How to join WINKT the club.

- Other fascinating books in the series.

- 'Houston – we MAY have a problem!'

- How to discover your family's history, coat of arms and the origin of your surname.

Index

MESSAGE FROM THE AUTHOR

Please help create a brand new word!

'Well I Never Knew That!' – the story so far

Back in Victorian Dublin a man bet that he could get everyone in Dublin using a brand new word within 24 hours. He won the bet by having four letters scrawled all over the walls that night. The next morning everyone pointed at the letters, said them out loud and said, 'What is that?' The letters were Q U I Z. He had created the word QUIZ, which we now use to describe competitions where someone says – 'What is …?'

I foolishly made a similar bet in a pub – to create a brand new word and to get it into the dictionary. This turned into a gargantuan project of tracking down and linking the most intriguing, fascinating and funniest origins of everyday phrases and names in the English language. All the boring ones have been thrown away! That's how this series of books came about!

When friends read the first book they often said 'Well, I never knew that!' – hence the name of the series. Then they shortened it to WINKT – the acronym of 'Well I Never Knew That!' meaning 'Wow!' or 'Gosh!' This is the new word: 'WINKT'!!!

'Please help finish the story!'

Now you've got WINKT the book – why not help create 'WINKT' the word and finish the story! All you have to do is send an email to word@winkt.com saying that 'I think "WINKT", meaning "Wow!" or "Gosh!" should be a new word in the dictionary.'

This will be added to the petition and when we get enough you will have played your part in creating a BRAND NEW WORD in the English language! In fact, if we get more than enough, we may even get into the *Guinness Book of World Records* as the most requested word ever! And, of course, tell your friends to email in as well. The more the merrier!

As a thank you I will give you free membership of WINKT the club!
Thank you,

Now you have enjoyed a WINKT book why not join WINKT the club?

As a member you can benefit from:

- Advance information on new books before they are generally available.

- Information on other WINKT products, cards, posters, etc.

- Beautiful manuscript-style scrolls that tell the professionally researched history and heritage of your family surname together with an historically accurate full-colour coat of arms. Fascinating and eye-catching presents, either framed or unframed. We can also offer a scroll with two coats of arms – ideal for a wedding or anniversary present.

- The opportunity to get your name into the credits of a future WINKT book by offering a new WINKT expression.

- A newsletter with more fascinating derivations, members' questions, competitions and prizes.

- Occasional emails sent to you with fascinating new WINKT origins.

- Sets of approved WINKT questions for use in pub/trivia quizzes, parties or dinner parties.

- 'Ask Peter' service for the derivation of specific words or phrases.

- Join the campaign to get 'WINKT' recognized as an official word and enter the Guinness Book of World Records to get the most requested word ever!

And much, much more.

Simply register online at www.WINKT.com and get your friends and family to register too! Join the fun today!

Recommended questions for Book Circles

'Well, I Never Knew That!' books are great for book circles because they can be read a little bit at a time, are such fun and always spark off interesting questions and discussions that can cause a real stir! For example:

- Which origins most surprised you?
- Which was your most 'WINKTASTIC' moment?
- How many times did you actually say 'Well, I never knew that!'?
- Who have you shared the WINKTs with and what was their reaction?
- How many times have you noticed people using the phrases since reading the book?
- What regional or family variations in phrases have you noticed?
- What must it be like for foreigners trying to learn English?
- What phrases or expressions used by other people really annoy you?
- What different nicknames do you use for family/friends or human anatomy?
- What phrases have been used in your family for years without anyone ever challenging what they really mean or why they exist?
- What new words or phrases do children bring back from school?
- What other phrases do you now want to know the origin of?

You can always log on to www.winkt.com and simply 'Ask Peter'.

And of course if you know a really interesting origin let Peter know so he can include it in a future book and include your name in the credits!

We love hearing from book circles and so, as a thank you, we offer special discounts for book-club orders. Log on to www.winkt.com to find out more.

Other books in the WINKT series

DID NOAH INVENT TENNIS?

AN HISTORIC MISCELLANY

Do you know ...

... why we score tennis 'love, 15, 30, 40, deuce'?

... why you had better 'cut to the chase', to avoid running 'from pillar to post'?

... why getting the 'sack' is better than being 'fired'?

... why the Battle of Agincourt was such a 'cock-up' for the French?

... why the 'exception' doesn't 'prove the rule' – and never did!

ISBN 0-9551525-1-8
ISBN 978-0-9551525-1-1

WHO PUT THE 'GREAT' IN GREAT BRITAIN?

THE HISTORY OF GREAT BRITAIN

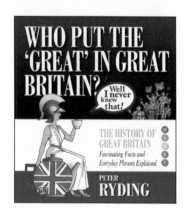

Do you know ...

... why England has three heraldic lions – because none of them was English!

... why Cromwell was such a 'whitewash', 'warts and all'?

... why we call our flag a 'Union JACK' – and why you may never have seen one?

... why a popular nursery rhyme teaches our children about destruction, boozing, pawning and child mortality? It's enough to make you 'pop your clogs'!

... and what is a 'cock-horse' anyway?

ISBN 0-9551525-3-4
ISBN 978-0-9551525-3-5

DID ROMANS DESIGN THE SPACE SHUTTLE?

THE ROMAN EMPIRE

Do you know ...

... how the Romans 'made a mint' when their city was destroyed?

... why they didn't just have vandals – they virtually invented them?

... how Roman sewers have helped specify modern trains and the Space Shuttle?

... why anyone paid a 'salary' owes it all to the Romans – especially if they are not 'worth their salt'?

... why the Romans gave us 'malaria'?

ISBN 0-9551525-5-0
ISBN 978-0-9551525-5-9

DID NELSON TURN A BLIND EYE?

NELSON AND THE ROYAL NAVY

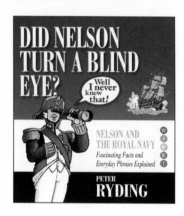

Do you know ...

... why letting 'the cat out of the bag' may leave you a 'marked man'?

... why the 'Jack and Jill' nursery rhyme is really about sex?

... why you must 'pull your finger out' before 'firing a broadside' at someone?

... why it doesn't hurt the 'monkey' when its balls are frozen off?

... the connection between shopping malls and the Battle of Trafalgar?

ISBN 0-9551525-2-6
ISBN 978-0-9551525-2-8

WHAT EVER HAPPENED TO OUR 27TH LETTER?

KNOWLEDGE, AND HOW WE USE IT!

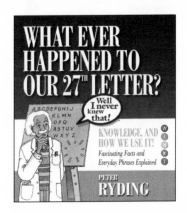

Do you know ...

... which flag gave bakers 13 to a dozen?

... why we all end sentences in Latin without even knowing it?

... what is the 27th letter of our alphabet?

... which idiot created fool's-cap paper and when did it become 'stationery'?

... how come the Sumerians gave us nothing but changed the world for ever?

ISBN 0-9551525-7-7
ISBN 978-0-9551525-7-3

Future WINKT books for release in 2007 and 2008

Log on to www.winkt.com to find out more.
Join the club and receive advance information of new releases!

- Time, Astronomy and Astrology
- Food and Drink
- London and Londoners
- Knights and Warfare through the Ages
- Big Business and Great Brands

- Ancient Greece
- USA and the World
- Cockney Rhyming Slang
- and more!

You've read the book – now play the game!

WELL I NEVER KNEW THAT – THE ADVENTURE!

The fun and fast-moving interactive **DVD** and **TV GAME** with fascinating and intriguing pictures, photos and video clues.

10 games on a DVD disc – guaranteed no repeat questions.

The perfect gift for lovers of words, phrases, history and our national heritage.

Available from www.winkt.com Autumn 2006.

Also by the same author

'Houston – we MAY have a problem!'

How to spot business issues early and fix them.

ISBN 0-9551525-9-3
ISBN 978-0-9551525-9-7

Copies can be ordered from www.peterryding.com

'I commend this book to anyone who feels they MAY be facing business challenges …
amusing and entertaining but without pulling any punches.'

SIR JOHN HARVEY-JONES MBE (of TV *Troubleshooter* fame)

'This short book is the most straightforward and digestible piece of commercial
education that I have come across.'

CHIEF EXECUTIVE OF THE SOCIETY OF TURNAROUND PROFESSIONALS

In the fast-paced business world of today everyone is under more stress than ever before. That includes CEOs and their directors. No wonder they need help. But how and when should they get that help?

This book provides the answer in a very short, illustrated and highly readable way. It is written by one of the UK's leading profit improvement experts and is specifically for CEOs and their leadership teams.

It tells the story of John, a CEO with a problem.

The trouble is, it has crept up on him and he doesn't know what to do.

'King Harold is too busy to see any salesmen right now.'

In fact, he doesn't really understand the severe implications for his business and for himself personally.

He then does the first of three critical things.

He gets help.

But is it too late?

If you haven't been there before, it is very tough to spot the problem, to identify which levers to pull, to know whom to believe and how to manage the various stakeholders around you. This book shows you what to do and what not to do.

'Reading this book could be the best spent thirty minutes of your career and save you a lot more than your job!'

SIR DIGBY JONES, DIRECTOR GENERAL OF THE CBI

To contact Peter please email peter@pathfinderpro.co.uk